W9-ABF-859

DO NOT
Leave Your Language Alone

The Hidden Status Agendas
Within Corpus Planning
in Language Policy

DO NOT
Leave Your Language Alone

The Hidden Status Agendas Within Corpus Planning in Language Policy

Joshua A. Fishman
Stanford University, California
New York University
Yeshiva University, New York

2006

LAWRENCE ERLBAUM ASSOCIATES, PUBLISHERS
Mahwah, New Jersey　　　　　　　　　　　London

Lawrence Erlbaum Associates, Inc., Publishers
10 Industrial Avenue
Mahwah, New Jersey 07430
www.erlbaum.com

Cover design by Tomai Maridou

Library of Congress Cataloging-in-Publication Data

Fishman, Joshua A.
Do not leave your language alone : the hidden status agendas within corpus planning in language policy / by Joshua A. Fishman.
p. cm.
Includes bibliographical references and index.
ISBN 0-8058-5023-6 (alk. paper)
ISBN 0-8058-5024-4 (pbk. : alk. paper)
1. Language planning. 2. Language policy. I. Title.
P40.5.L35F57 2006
306.44'9—dc22 2005054160
CIP

Books published by Lawrence Erlbaum Associates are printed on acid-free paper, and their bindings are chosen for strength and durability.

Printed in the United States of America
10 9 8 7 6 5 4 3 2 1

For three guardian angels, Gella (first and foremost for well over half a century), Guadalupe and Chris, all of whom were available at the drop of a hat and without whose help this volume could simply not have been completed.
"Peace unto you, oh guardian angels!"

For Elissa, whom I love so dearly and who knows full well that the most important care of all, for children as for languages, is offered by those who love them unconditionally.

פֿאַר אַלע שומרי־ייִדיש באמונה־שלמה, ווייניק אין כמות נאָר גרויס אין איכות.

Contents

Preface

In earlier and more innocent times, it was widely believed that language, just as any other gift from God, could neither be "planned" nor "improved". As those times were coming to an end, an attempt was made by Professor Robert A. Hall (1950) to foster the complete disappearance of language planning by harsh criticism, discouraging scholarly activity in the language-planning direction. His book, *Leave Your Language Alone!*, now stands as a monument to a bygone age. Today, the wheel has turned once more, as wheels are supposed to do, and scholarly books on language planning are more likely, by far, to consider how to intervene, whether in the language change process itself (all living languages change, with or without human intervention, over time), or, even more so, in the functions (or "uses" and "purposes") to which particular languages are put within the speech and writing communities of their users.

It is difficult to say which of these two approaches to "language problems" is the more difficult for most humans: not to intervene at all or to do so wisely and effectively in a world brim full of unanticipated and often undesirable consequences. But, in any case, the Rubicon has been crossed and it is no longer possible to put "the toothpaste back into the tube". Languages are increasingly viewed as scarce national resources (not unlike flora and fauna, agricultural or environmental resources, and all other such improvable or alterable resources whose quality can be influenced by planned human intervention). Speech and writing communities the world over are not only expected to exert themselves on behalf of their own languages, but to feel remiss if they fail to do so when their language resources are threatened.

In fact, this slim volume tackles only part of the entire language-planning flowchart. Indeed, it sets "status planning" aside (on the grounds that there are by now several perfectly acceptable treatments of that aspect of the flowchart; e.g., see Fishman, 2001 for a comparative examination of some 20 different cases drawn from different continents) in order to focus entirely on corpus planning. There are at least two good reasons for doing so. First of all, I am convinced that the two types of language planning are not as fundamentally separate as has traditionally been assumed to be the case, and, second, that the nature and direction of corpus planning per se reflects and is guided by the status-planning environment—societal biases, ideologies and attitudes—in which it is conducted. Thus, it is not the case that status-planning factors are being ignored in this volume, but, rather, that their nature, direction, and power cannot be fully, productively, or systematically explored head-on, that is, in isolation from the corpus-planning influences with which they are inevitably intertwined.

Language planning is ultimately judged not by its small coterie of specialized language planners but, most crucially, by its intended consumers. The same is true for textbooks vis-à-vis their authors and readers. It is my hope that this brief introductory treatment of the largely underplayed corpus planning aspect of language planning will be looked upon favorably by students and instructors, at least in the near future, that is, until once again, the human mind discovers the inevitable— that there is still more unexplored variance in this topic.

I would be remiss not to mention, at least briefly, a secondary goal that has figured in my writing this text, namely, to help students become more aware of the variety of language communities in the world, even now, when globalization seems to rule the roost. I would dearly love our students to grasp the variety of the historical experiences of language situations, their relationships to each other and, particularly, the variety of their expectations and hopes vis-à-vis language planning. One of the severest penalties exacted from English mother-tongue speakers, for their unchallenged position in the world of power and possessions, is their distinctly "handicapped" status insofar as appreciating a world of many cultures, peoples, nations, ethnicities, and languages. It has fallen to sociolinguists to attempt to rise to the latter challenge as much as to the former one. Within the limits of a one semester course, I have tried to teach (and to write) about corpus planning in a way that would help familiarize college-age individuals with the still huge variation in human characteristics that inevitably influences (and that will long, long continue to do so, with or without globalization) the reception and the direction that corpus planning receives and takes.

For those who still shake their heads astoundedly at the "spectacle" of serious societal contortions on behalf of their small, weak, little known, and, seemingly, very forgettable languages, it is a prerequisite of a productive life in the modern world to set aside Olympian detachment or disdain for the unfortunate and to at least strive toward critical identification with all those who think as much (as often, as deeply, as concernedly), if not more, of their languages of minor reach as we think of our huge one. Critical identification with that huge segment of humanity with which we have no direct kinship ties is a vital part of genuine, activated, emotional, and intellectual modernization of our students and it is my sincere hope that this brief exercise will contribute to that goal both directly and indirectly via an "excursion" taking only a month or two.

I recognize fully that this short and, at times, lighthearted treatment (after all, corpus planning need not be a somber and lugubrious affair in order to be taken seriously) is not the last word on its topic and I now place it before the many readers and critics who have so often in the past also been my teachers and guides.

Joshua A. Fishman
Spring 2005
Stanford University
(www.JoshuaAFishman.com)

REFERENCES

Fishman, J. A. (Ed.). (2001). *Can threatened languages be saved?* Clevedon: Multilingual Matters.
Hall, R. A. (1950). *Leave your language alone!* Ithaca: Linguistica.

1

Introduction to Language Planning: Some Preliminaries

"TO MEET THE KING OF PERSIA AND TO BE HIS WIFE"[1]

Do you remember the bible's Book of Esther? Since you are interested in language planning, you may want to go back and read it again (or even read it for the first time). It is not only a brief and exciting story, which includes a beauty contest to find a new Queen for the great King of Persia and Media (whose empire is said to have spread from India to Ethiopia), but it also contains explicit references to a very modern and multicultural language policy for those ancient times. When the mighty Ahasuerus sought to notify the people in the many provinces of his decision to choose a new queen, based on a criterion of beauty alone, he sent news of an impending beauty contest for this very purpose to all corners of the far-reaching empire consisting of over 127 provinces and even more "peoples". And how was the news delivered by swift runners, dispatched in every direction, in order to make the king's plans known far and wide? The text tells us that letters were sent: "into every province according to the writing thereof, and to every people after their language" (Esther 1:23 King James Version).

---

[1]From a children's play commonly performed when celebrating Purim (commemorating the biblical Queen Esther and King Ahasuerus).

Evidently, there were both written languages and strictly oral languages in the huge empire. Those who could read the local language could be reached by means of posters affixed to walls and poster boards near all major points of congregation; however, those that could not read, or who spoke only unwritten languages, had to have the king's proclamation read out to them in the vernacular of the local people. If current circumstances are any indication of how matters were then, there were probably many more illiterates than literates and more unwritten languages than written ones. Nevertheless, the king wanted all to be informed of his plans, without regard to social class, race, religion, or ethnicity. The policy in force must have been an expensive one, even though it only provided for one direction of communication, namely, from the "center" to the "periphery". In that direction, all languages, written or unwritten, were considered equal for the receipt of an urgent message from the king. This is an instance of language status policy. Had there been a deliberative legislative body at the time, some legislator might have contested the political wisdom, that is, the "efficacy for reaching desired goals" or of attaining a "positive cost-benefit ratio" of proceeding in this fashion. Some might have suggested concentrating only on the largest languages, written or spoken, on the theory that most of those who didn't know them as first languages would know them as second or third languages (or could easily find someone to read and translate the proclamation for them).

Indeed, some of the largest languages of Persia and Media were cross-border languages and some xenophobic legislator might have argued that any information conveyed via these languages would quickly reach hostile ears and would constitute a security risk. Thus the allocation of the status of being "a language of government" as cavalierly as the king seems to have done, could well have been a mistake, or regarded as such. Nevertheless, it is an example of status planning, one of the two major types of language planning that have gone on all over the world for thousands of years. It encompasses reaching decisions as to the particular societal functions that languages might have: for example, approval (from the "authorities") that a language can/should be used (or, conversely, prohibited) in the courts, or in education, or in hospitals, or in the armed forces, or in police and fire services, or in large and small businesses, or on traffic signs, or in houses of worship, or in the official work of the legislative and executive branches, or in elections and voting, or in the disbursement of funds, and so forth. All of these are examples of possible arenas of status planning. Language status decisions are not necessarily all made by governmental authorities, although many are, particularly if they pertain to functions at the highest levels of power and symbolic significance. We will return to this topic from time to time later, although, quite frankly, it is not exactly the major focus of this book.

Corpus Planning

The other major type of language planning, *corpus planning*, is probably of equal or greater vintage than the status planning that we have discussed thus far. What would the scribes of King Ahasuerus have done if there were no word for "beauty contest" in many of the languages that they were obliged to use? Or suppose the speakers of certain hitherto oral languages had long been clamoring for a written form. Even if approved, this requires decisions with respect to (a) the creation of a writing system (e.g., should it be Latin-based or Arabic-based, a matter of considerable recent political significance in the case of Somali); (b) an authoritative spelling (or "orthographic") system (e.g., "colour" and "labour" or "color" and "labor", the former duo as in Australian and Canadian English, both of which have come to require dictionaries separate from those for British or American English) (c) a style manual to establish conventions for capitalization and hyphenation; (d) a terminology for all or at least some of the major natural sciences (how would Gandhi have said "ferric sulfate" as distinct from "ferric sulfide"?, and so forth. All in all, corpus planning is crucially important for "developing languages" that are also attempting to interact (i.e., to encourage interaction on the part of their speakers and writers) with the modern world , whether for commercial, touristic, political, and/or educational purposes. But we mustn't think that developing languages are the only ones that need to or that seek to "tamper" with their language.

Corpus planning is ongoing also in the case of English. The use of "Ms". in addressing or mentioning females without making reference to their marital status is less than half a century old in English. In the United States, it was strongly advocated by the National Organization of

Women (NOW), an organization that also strongly opposed "androcentric pronouns" ("Whoever is the last person to leave the room, would <u>he</u> please shut off the lights?") and "androcentric occupational terms" (mail<u>man</u>, congress<u>man</u>, fire<u>man</u>, weather<u>man</u>, etc.). Clearly, however, although both status planning and corpus planning with respect to the "gendering" of English have obviously occurred, the kinds of social problems (and, therefore, the kinds of status planning), the kinds of language authorities, and the kinds of sanctions available to enforce language decisions can be, as one might expect, far different in the socioauthoritative bodies that operate at far different points along the political continuum and the continuum of proximity to the political movers and shakers above them.

Three W Words (When?, Why?, Where?) and One H Word (How?) in Connection With Corpus Planning

The most common prod to corpus planning is a noticeable change that is desired or that has transpired in status planning. Corpus planning corresponds to two widespread convictions: that language usage helps bring about social change, on one hand and that language usage helps reinforce or stabilize social change, on the other hand. Kamil Pasha Ataturk adopted a Western (i.e., a Romanized writing system and a compulsory standardized spelling therein) for Turkish, in 1932) as part of his more general program to modernize and Westernize hitherto "Ottoman" Turkey, the so-called "sick man of Europe". He conceived of this wholesale and totally obligatory switch as a means of attaining the Europeanization that he advocated and as a means of cementing or enforcing that change vis-à-vis subsequent generations. Sometimes corpus change is a byproduct of prior status change decisions (as in Ataturk's case) and, sometimes, it is a tool for bringing social change and, therefore, status change into being (e.g., the conversion of Moldavian, hitherto written in Latin characters (like Roumanian) into Cyrillic characters (like Russian) after the discontinuation of the post- World War II Soviet occupation). However, in either case, whether corpus planning is engaged to undertake social change or to reinforce the longevity of social change that is already underway, it is desirable for these two activities (corpus and status planning) to go on simultaneously (or almost so), it should be clear that language planning is part of the total social change (social planning) process, whether as cause and/or as effect.

Why is this so? Because social change consists of change(s) at the individual, local, regional, and/or national levels. These circumstances need to be written about, fostered, opposed, taught about in schools, legislated about, codified, and all of the above require precise and consensual usage for effective communication to be brought about. Human problem solving per se and societal problem solving even more so are highly language-dependent activities. Such dependence makes it imperative that a consensus be arrived at quickly as to which language should be utilized for which functions and how this language should become part of the written record and, thereby, accessible to the popular press, to academic textbooks at all levels, to legal or medical databanks, and to retrieval systems more generally. Thus, social change per se also entails language change that is appropriate to that change (or, conversely, to undo that change). Of course, not all efforts on behalf of social change succeed and, therefore, much language planning is not only done, but undone and redone, as different and differing regimes and their respective language authorities come into and go out of power. We do not envy the poor Moldavians who have gone from no writing system at all to a Latin-based writing system, to a Cyrillic based writing system, to a Latin-based one again (this time, one that is indistinguishable in writing from Romanian), all within less than a century. A great deal of successively contradictory language planning (as was not uncommon under the Soviets) is always indicative of contradictory and repetitive political changes (or approaches to changes) in the culture as a whole.

Language planning is always done in accord with the more general culture of planning (agricultural planning, industrial planning, educational planning, etc.) insofar as the need for consensus building and the use of sanctions (negative or positive) are concerned. Ataturk and the Soviets severely punished opponents of the "official" orthographies and nomenclatures that their respective language planners introduced and legislated (see, e.g., Landau, 1993, Hornjatkjevyč, 1993). Similarly, Turkish and Soviet cultures of planning and their associated cultures of sanctions were each far different during the mid and late 1920s than those obtaining in the United States and England at the end of that same century, with respect to those who insisted on continuing to use the old androcentric titles and terms.

However, there is one way in which language planning is quite similar cross-culturally and that pertains to its primary stress on the formal (educated) and primarily written (or literary) language, as distinct from the informal spoken varieties. Generally, whatever impact language planning has on the spoken language is derivative, that is, it derives from the impact of formal writing on formal speech. Such an impact will obviously obtain to the greatest degree in the speech of social and educational groups that are most exposed to education in general and involved in reading and formality in particular. When mother-tongue teachers express their disappointment with the "unschoolworthiness" of their students' written and spoken usage (a common complaint heard round the world today), they are really revealing the paucity of their students' reading under the onslaught of a modern, worldwide youth culture that is purportedly based primarily on television, recordings, and face-to-face interaction. Of course, this interdependence can be overdone. Some university professors (no names mentioned!) have been known to "speak too bookishly" (at least insofar as a particular situation is concerned, such as advising friends who are examining the paintings in his study to "kindly extinguish all illumination prior to vacating the premises"). Others, less familiar with the spoken language that is their medium of instruction than they are with its written version, engage in "spelling pronunciations" (e.g., pronouncing the second "l" in Lincoln or the "b" in subtle). All in all, however, the impact of language planning is far weaker vis-à-vis the spoken language than it is on the written/printed version. Why should that be?

The Written Standard

There is a simple reason why language planning in general and corpus planning in particular aim more explicitly at the written (actually, usually the printed) language than at its spoken counterpart. Language in print is more nearly controllable and rewardable because it can be monitored by schools, editors, publishers, and/or governmental review boards. The written language often has, or develops, an identifiable standard to which it can be compared and held. Writing is a more con-

sciously deliberate activity than speaking and therefore there is more
self-correction (a type of individual language planning) in writing and,
therefore, more of a possibility of replacing the spontaneous and informal spoken language by a more educated (if not exactly more formal)
variety of the language. Those who do most of the writing are themselves likely to be most educated and, having spent more years in school
and more time reading, they are likely to have been more influenced by
teachers and others acting *"in loco authoritatus"*.

It is an unstated and often even unconscious rule in all languages everywhere that no one writes exactly as they speak (the great Vuk
Stefanovič Karadzić, 1787–1864, to the contrary notwithstanding)[2] and
that no one speaks exactly the way they write (not even Harvard professors). Or to put it another way, even the speech of educated people reveals, at least here and there, the dialect area and the social circles in
which they grew up, even when it is not the language variety of the
school. Nevertheless, it is the written standard (or lacking that, the formal spoken variety) that becomes symbolic of the highest dignity of the
people as a body, just as does its flag. It is this variety (of literature, of
law, of religion, of education, and of cultured society more generally)
that the authorities succeed most in molding, almost regardless of what
is transpiring "on the street". This variety, of course, is not frozen, not
fixed for all eternity, but neither is it subject to constant major influences
from popular songs and adolescent slang.

When some of his earliest supporters tried to get Eliezer ben Yehuda
(1858–1922), the so-called "father" of the revernacularization of Hebrew, some 2000 years after it had ceased to be the language of daily informal speech, to give his stamp of approval to a term already being used
by the common folk in the marketplace, his reply was, significantly,
"Why should I care what they are saying in the marketplace?" Thus does
an "image of the best language" impose itself on the work of authorities.
However much "the best language" may be defined, however much it
may be subject to deeply held (and strongly biased) political preferences (about which we will have a great deal to say in the chapters to fol-

---

[2]In his efforts to spread literacy in modern Serbian, Vuk Karadzić advised the "man in the street" to
"write as you speak." He was not, however, advocating the use of vulgarisms or defective sentences
(both common characteristics of much popular speech) as much as the appropriateness of departing
from Old Serbian Church Slavonic when writing the modern language (see Fig. 1.1).

FIG 1.1. The famous Vuk. His advice: "Write as you speak."

low), however much it is a flexible construct that can be guided in one way or another, after all is said and done, a notion of what is "best" underlies corpus planning as a whole and the written variety in particular. This may at times require a choice between two languages (e.g., a religious language vs. a workaday one), or, at times, the choice between one closer to a given dialect than to another (e.g., the Yiddish of the northern Eastern European regions [Lithuania and Belarus] vs. the Yiddish of the more central and southerly regions [Central Poland and the Ukraine]). However, once this choice is made (admittedly, for ideological reasons) or a compromise between them is fashioned, it is the written variety of "the chosen" that will be most impacted by corpus planning, particularly the planning for high status purposes.[3]

Conclusions

We have learned in this chapter that language planning is subdivisible into two large components: status planning and corpus planning, The two are linked in many ways that we examine in chapter 2. We have also seen that both types of language planning are put on a language community's agenda when societal change is prominent, problem-solving is vital, and a premium is paid for communication ease and consensual clarity of meaning. Finally, we have learned that corpus planning is primarily aimed at (and evaluated in terms of the widespread adoption of its impact upon) the variety of the language most associated with formal, high-status use. In modern societies, this is most likely to be the written language, that is, the type of language most easily and most frequently monitored by and influenced by language authorities as well as the type most likely to become symbolic of (and, therefore, most valued by) the language community itself.

Language planning, of one kind or another, will vary in the emphases and resources devoted to it. Language planning often continues on, in a much lower key, even after the periods of most pressing social change

---

[3]None of the foregoing is meant to imply that there is no language planning at all for oral languages. Classical Koranic Arabic was probably standardized orally by court poets attached to local chieftains, even before the Koran was "received". However, this does not violate the rule that the variety that is intended for formal, high-status functions is the one that receives most authoritative corpus-planning attention.

have passed, to recover something of the prior prominence of a language if such pressures for social change resume in that direction. The ever-present linkage between corpus planning and other major cultural trends and processes becomes (part of) the basis of local "linguistic culture" (Schiffman, 1996), that is, part of widespread convictions as to what is "good" or "bad" (acceptable or unacceptable) in polite company. In so far as corpus planning is concerned, linguistic culture consists of refinements and reformulations of folk legends, folk memories, folk heroes, and proto-ideology. The ordinary educated folks accept these and give folk-linguistics more credence than even its initiators may ever have intended.

The constant corpus-planning focus on the written language also stimulates and fosters both the confirmation or the disconfirmation of the notions about language that the local "linguistic culture" has suggested. Furthermore, the written language cannot but influence the spoken language too, particularly among those most immersed in the written language. It is difficult, under such circumstances to find and to keep to a reliable border between "incorrect" spelling pronunciations and the norms that corpus planning genuinely supports.[4]

REFERENCES AND FURTHER READINGS

Fishman, J. A., & Cobarrubias, J. C. (Eds.). (1983). *Progress in language planning*. Berlin: Mouton.

Hornjatkjevyč, A. (1993). The 1928 Ukrainian orthography. in J. A. Fishman (Ed.), *The earliest stage of language planning* (pp. 293–304). Berlin: Mouton.

Landau, J. (1993). The first Turkish language congress. In J. A. Fishman (Ed.), *The earliest stage of language planning* (pp. 271–292). Berlin: Mouton.

Schiffman, H. (1996). *Linguistic culture and language policy*. New York: Routledge.

---

[4]Note that Appendix 1 contains a discussion question to be answered orally and/or in writing, as you instructor directs. There is one such question for each chapter.

2

Corpus Planning and Status Planning: Separates, Opposites, or Siamese Twins?

The distinction seems so elementary, so why belabor it? *Corpus planning* has to do with authoritative efforts on behalf of the characteristics of a language per se and *status planning* has to do with the societal functions of the language to which the authorities aspire, right? Only partially right, because such a simplistic view leaves unanswered many questions about either one and also implies a higher degree of unrelatedness between the two than is actually the case. Life is complicated and so is language planning with its many alternative ins and outs.

SEPARATENESS AND SEQUENCING

If the two parts of language planning are really separate from each other, then this raises the question, "With which one of these two does the total process begin?" Each of the two obviously possible answers to this question (three, if you opt for a simultaneous beginning on both fronts) has been given due consideration by students of language planning. I am somewhat embarrassed to admit it, but I myself have held all three views (fortunately, at different times, rather than simultaneously).

The supporters of primacy for status planning reason as follows: Without a status issue on the horizon, what conceivable use would corpus planning be? If the issue of Polish independence (particularly from Russia) were not so overriding, then what would have been the motor to lead Poles toward adopting an essentially Roman alphabet (as well as Roman Catholicism, rather than Eastern Catholicism, unlike most other Slavs)? If it were not so as to facilitate their becoming "masters of their own house", would Franco–Canadians have begun their own language planning agency (*Service de la Langue Francaise*)? If it were not in order to involve Indonesians in auxiliary activities required by the Japanese occupation of Indonesia during World War II, would the Japanese authorities have permitted and created the Indonesian Language Board? If it were not for the sake of facilitating the creation of a Jewish state in Palestine, would Eliezer ben Yehuda have established the Academy of the Hebrew Language toward the end of the 19th century? If it were not necessary to reinforce the newly gained American independence from Great Britain, would Noah Webster have authored a speller and a grammar of the "American language" and petitioned congress for the establishment of a federal academy for that very purpose? It was only after the independence of the Philippines and after the proclamation of Pilipino (a puristically defined variety of the Tagolog of the Manila region, minus the foreignisms and barbarisms of the latter) as its national language, that a language agency was established to modernize and to "intellectualize" the language, so that it could better serve to unify a modern nation. In general, wherever the state comes into existence prior to the beginning of language planning, it may make better sense to start with corpus planning, because most of the more urgent status goals have already been attained and the language has, therefore, already been recognized for governmental, school, media, and court use. The major problem faced by Pilipino, for example, was that no one knew exactly what it was or exactly how to speak or write it. There were no teachers who could utilize it as language of instruction or even target of instruction. There were no textbooks published in Pilipino as yet. Without some very effective corpus planning immediately, it was easy to see that either Pilipino was headed for trouble or, at the least, it was going to drop from visibility by dint of its own shortcomings due to insufficient advanced planning (see chap. 4, this volume to find out what really happened).

The sensibility of the aforementioned sequence (status planning first and corpus planning later) is quite apparent. Status rewards, goals, and possibilities are powerful motivators, not only materially but also culturally and socially. However, it is always dangerous to reach an "obvious" conclusion, particularly when there is a danger of being prematurely persuaded to ignore much evidence to the contrary.

Efforts to modernize Estonian began well before the liberation of Estonia from Czarist Russian rule. Pompeo Fabra began his efforts to standardize Catalan spelling and grammar well before the proclamation of Catalan autonomy during the brief period of the pre-Franco Spanish Republic. The same is the case for Basque. In Spain (i.e., in Castilla per se) Antonio de Nebrija (1444–1522) urged the establishment of an Academia Reál de la Lengua, prior to the discovery of the New World (1492) with all its untold riches for the King's coffers, but not till 1713 did this come to pass. Certainly the process of standardizing English and German via great dictionaries seems to have benefitted little from any status rewards (either for the countries or lexicographers involved) on the horizon. Corpus planning for Italian began with the famous "mother of all academies", *Accademia dela Crusca* (1582), which was established centuries before the unification of Italy (or of Italian either). Even Cardinal Richelieu's *Academie Francaise* (1635) was established "only" in order that France's "letters be held in honor as well as its arms", rather than to amplify a larger, all-purpose corpus for the language (see Fig. 2.1 and Fig. 2.2).

Having mentioned many of the great European languages as examples of the "corpus planning first" camp, we must also mention in this camp all of the nonstate languages of Europe and elsewhere. None of them start off with any already existing status advantage which could stimulate corpus planning thereafter. Neither Occitan, nor Frisian, nor Rusyn, nor Komi started their corpus planning efforts from prior positions of status strength. Indeed, the prior lack of status strength may be the common feature characterizing the corpus planning of all suppressed or disadvantaged languages everywhere. They begin where they can! Perhaps, tinkering with the language proper is less likely to elicit the opposition, much less the wrath, of the superordinate authorities by which they are surrounded and controlled. Not every language can have a state, but many, many more languages can have a lexicogra-

FIG. 2.1. Entrance to the Academie Francaise.

FIG. 2.2.   Coat of Arms of the Spanish Royal Academy (1713), with
Inscription "Pure, Permanent, and Providing Splendor."

pher, a grammarian, a stylist who undertake their labor of love without anything more material than ethnocultural self-respect in mind. The pre-World War I Austro-Hungarian monarchy is a case in point. Although it long had only German and Hungarian as its official languages, it was a veritable hotbed of language planning toward the end of the 19th century (Polish, Serbian, Slovene, Croatian, Ukrainian, Rusyn, Yiddish, etc.) for its many "non-state languages". Lack of superordinate power is a powerful motivator for starting language planning from the corpus planning end and to "go slow" with any status planning that can upset the powers that be. In the absence of clear status prospects, corpus is all that most latecomers to modernity and/or independence have to work on.

So, how does that leave the simultaneity option? Viewing status planning and corpus planning as "two sides of the same [language planning] coin" is an appealing metaphor. Certainly, it is good advice. It implies that it doesn't do for one phase to be seriously out of touch with the other, neither too far in advance of the other, nor lagging woefully behind the other. If new statuses (e.g., the authorization of funding to teach the natural sciences at university level in Basque, Irish, or Frisian) do not quickly acquire new authoritative corpuses of their own, then they are left with no options other than either to borrow what they lack from more advanced neighbors, or, for those involved daily in these new statuses, to amateurishly "repair the gaps" (often without any coordination among them), as they move along. The first approach might have us all still using German today in our science labs and classrooms, since German was the stellar "language of science" in the 19th century), while the second would result in a surfeit of ad hoc "patches", which could very well become barriers to further scientific progress. The advice that we should develop both "sides" of the language planning process in close tandem with one another is certainly good advice, but good advice is not what we lack. "Good advice" deals with what should be done, not with what inevitably must be done. At any rate, this advice reveals the weakness in the "two sides of the same coin" metaphor, since a coin must have two sides because "you can't have one without the other". The metaphor implies much more automatic synchronicity than actually obtains. In actuality, language planning is usually a "catch-up" undertaking with respect to the sequencing of its two parts. The intervals between the stages are by no means equal and, as Fig. 2.3 shows:

```
Conf . . . >
SP3-->SP1--->CP1-------->SP2------>SP4----------CP2--->SP6---> SP5
...................................................................
```

FIG. 2.3.   Unequalness of intervals and irregularity of sequencing in language planning.

We may agree that in a perfect world, status planning and corpus planning would be carefully integrated with and well attuned to each other, but language planning does not exist within anything approaching a perfect world, but, rather, in a world that is not only imperfect but submerged in political and economic stresses and strains. Welcome to the real world! In the real world, status planning and corpus planning are more detached and isolated from each other than they should be from the point of view of optimal progress. But history is far from being directionally predictable, much less controllable, and these truisms too keep corpus planning and status planning from usually being just two sides of one and the same coin.

Conclusions

Language planning *en toto* and each of its subparts individually are much too complex and much too dictated by history to be independently or jointly predicted with any comforting degree of accuracy. The total process neither necessarily starts with nor ends with any particular subpart, handy metaphors to the contrary notwithstanding. Where it starts, when it starts, and in which way it develops is determined by the context—political, economic, cultural—in which it develops. This should not be a discouraging realization. Cultures differ widely throughout the world. They stress different values, priorities and goals vis-à-vis language (Schiffman, 1996) as well as everyday life. If there is any parsimony to understanding language planning, it exists within the certainty that it corresponds in many crucial ways to the state of the culture that elicits and nurtures it.

REFERENCE

Schiffman, H. (1996). *Linguistic culture and language planning*. New York: Routledge.

3

The Directions
and Dimensions
of Corpus Planning

While it is undoubtedly true that status planning and corpus planning can be linked in a variety of sequences, it is also the case that sequencing ("which comes first ... ?") is not itself a matter into which planners *per se* have much input. Nor does it inform their work. Nor is it what is on the minds of their sponsors when the latter commission (or command) corpus planning to proceed. The directional forces moving and guiding corpus planning are more political, ideological, or value laden and far more specific along those very lines, going far beyond the specificity or monodirectionality of such major outcome goals as "modernization".

One can become modern in many different ways. Modernity can be pursued by breaking entirely with the recent past, as did Ataturk when he adopted a Western ("European", Latin based) writing system and discarded the Ottoman style of Arabic writing (Ossmanli) that the Turks had used for centuries. Or modernization can be pursued in a fashion that stresses "authenticity" or continuity with the past, in fact or in fancy, as Japanese modernizers have long done. What's the difference which way one does it, as long as the outcome is the same—modernization? Actually, there may be quite a difference insofar as the perception of locals is concerned and it is their perception (or the perception of the "authorities" among them) that determines the success or failure [adoption or nonadoption] of the corpus innovations being recommended. The Turkish approach may leave a tear in the societal fabric, one that cannot be completely healed for generations, between rapid and slow modernizers in the population. The wholesale adoption of "Westernisms" (a term which is merely a cover word for "Americanisms" in the present) may introduce a legion of recognizably "different" terms (or even grammatical choices such as the leveling of prior honorific options), differences that are easily recognizable by one and all and that may therefore come to stand for the hated enemy rather than just for a higher standard of indigenous living and a consensually modified consumer culture.

In an age of globalization, when a single language, culture, and lifestyle are constantly spreading from one continent to the next, the very notion of modernization may represent a serious dilemma for the local authorities and for the rank-and-file members. Modernization may be met with considerable ambivalence, whether it is the verbal or the material culture that is involved. Corpus change also involves and reflects ongoing sociocultural change and there is no cultural change that does not harm the prerogatives of at least some proportion of the population. Even easing the spread of adult literacy may endanger established social class privileges, or gender privileges, or age privileges. Depending on the corpus planning that accompanies (and comes to characterize and to foster) ongoing sociocultural change, the newly literate may come to lose the key to their own, ancient, differently written literature, or they may come to gain entrée to the literature of neighboring but heretofore hostile cultures of similar speech but of a differing religious persuasion (which also implies that the latter are now more open to the printed matter of the former), more open to cross-border trade (legal or not), more eager to acquire word processors using the writing-system of the foreigners, more exposed to the World Wide Web and all of its portals to forbidden sights and delights. No wonder that not all of the world welcomes corpus planning with open arms.

Is there then no compromise, no halfway house, no internal screening process via which "good modernization" can be admitted and "bad modernization" can be excluded? That would be very fine and good, but it is a solution that is very hard to come by (try applying it to the World Wide

Web!) and, furthermore, one person's "compromise" is viewed as a "capitulation" by another. Or, what is widely viewed as an acceptable compromise at time A is no longer viewed as such in time B (due to the outbreak of regional hostilities, increasing trade imbalances, growing fundamentalism at home and/or abroad, etc.). The world is becoming more and more polarized as globalization marches ahead and is perceived as a welcome change by some, as an unwelcome intruder by others, and as both the one and the other by still others. The result is that although nearly all sides engage in modernization to some degree, the degree and the kind of modernization is closely scrutinized as is the degree and kind of corpus planning that will meet least opposition and have the fewest unintended side effects or linkages. Such efforts clearly reveal the nature and degree of the political and ideological encumberedness of corpus planning. Verily: there is no (and can be no) politically innocent or value-free corpus planning.

In that case, must all corpus planning be seen as part of a plot or conspiracy to transfer power to one party or another? This may be so, but in that case, the anticorpus planners must also be seen as defending a vested interest of their own. The redistribution of privilege and the retention or expansion of privilege may not be morally equivalent, but neither is there any camp totally devoid of self-interest. How could there be? Human societies are a means by which their members organize to obtain those rewards (spiritual and material) that they prize. Although everyone prizes a good meal and a clean bed, even such minimal physical essentials reveal a huge disparity in how they are defined, the priority that is placed upon them, and the means that are culturally approved for attaining them. Therefore, it should come as no surprise that there is an even greater disparity of views and values when we approach the much more complex set of means and ends that are involved in corpus planning. And yet, there is hardly a human aggregate that does not engage in corpus planning at one time or another; therefore, it behooves us to learn to recognize how corpus planning helps attain goals and express values in an age of rapid globalization such as ours.

Of course, globalization too receives a mixed press. As a result, corpus planning can be utilized to resist and to temper globalization, rather than merely to facilitate and advance it. The Missouri Baptist Synod does not use corpus planning in its bible translations in the same way or for the same purposes that the Unitarian Church does. Most striking of all, however, is the human ability to mask one goal via stressing another. Corpus planning provides us with opportunities to note that kind of ploy as well.

But why try to disguise one's attempts to "handle" globalization, whether one's views toward it are positive or negative? Because many authorities are really ambivalent or conflicted with respect to globalization. They both love it and hate it simultaneously. Ultra-religious authorities may claim that they hate it (because it serves as a purveyor of pornography, Western materialism, and the denial of God's rule over all and everything), but they also know that they want it because it provides access to other Western products such as a vastly superior constructive and destructive econotechnology. Once such goods are admitted, locals must be trained to use them, repair them, and, at times, even to buy them from or sell them to other locals. The opposite scenario obtains when thoroughly pro-Western authorities must contend with a strongly entrenched ultra-fundamentalist opposition. The result in both cases may be quite similar as far as corpus planning for the local national language is concerned (so that it can be easily, rigorously, and productively employed in conjunction with the pursuit of certain desired end products of globalization). Retaining an ancient indigenous writing system is a very powerful symbol in itself, for clothing ["packaging"] globalization in an indigenous garb of traditional lore and amenities. If that can be done, the next huge task is to create local terminologies that utilize native roots, prefixes, suffixes, plurals, and syntactic order. Accomplishing all of this is a tall order for corpus planners, but may well be considered well worth the cost if a compromise solution to the direction of corpus planning is a vital desideratum. Of course, like many compromises that most of us have experienced, it leaves no one completely satisfied and provides corpus planners with two groups of adversaries instead of only one: adversaries to the left of them (who are adamant for full scale, visible, and rapid globalization, on one hand) and adversaries to the right of them (who are adamant for preserving the language and the culture in their "original" pristine and sacred states).

There is still another compromise, namely one which permits only a trusted and carefully screened econotechnical elite to have "access to globalization via it's own language(s)". This approach, of course, does not really require much corpus planning for the indigenous language, but it engenders steep costs of its own, because it gives rise to a whole host of regulatory procedures and authoritative boundary strengthening policies that are entirely foreign to and outside of corpus planning per se.

Conclusions

The ideological direction pursued by corpus planning is fully in accord with the authoritative ideological direction more generally. It would not do for corpus planning to be globalization positive while the political and cultural elite are mainly globalization negative and preoccupied with recovering and fostering the local, classical past. Whereas "globalization positive" and "globalization negative" are handy abstractions for describing the two major directions in corpus planning, they are not sufficiently precise to differentiate between subtypes within each of these camps. In the chapters that follow, some of this differentiation is illustrated and then the issues of consistency and reliability is addressed both within and between the subtypes.

4

Purity Versus Vernacularity: Does "Folksiness" Come Before or After "Cleanliness"?

There is a widespread popular assumption that proper languages are "clean" or "pure". Generally this means that each of them is of a single parentage or provenance. However, because this so popular an assumption, language planners often attempt to capitalize on it and to seek to persuade their target populations that any linguistic innovation is totally in accord with (i.e., has the same word formation as, or the same sound sequencing as is common in) that in the main body of the language. Whatever is new, according to the principle of purity, must be seamless with the old and cannot be visible within it nor does it depart from it. Actually, "purity" may be more honored in theory than in practice, probably because it is usually far more attainable in theory than in practice.

Of course, for purity to be attainable at all, the "opponent(s)" must be made palpably recognizable and, indeed, even easily detectable. Such recognizability must not be limited only to the recondite circles of linguists, language activists, or language planners more specifically, but must be made palpably clear and instantly recognizable, and to the public of native speakers at large, rather than just to the educated elites, so that ordinary folk too can join in the hunt for "foreignisms" that need to be exposed and guarded against. However, any such goal is more easily set than met.

Among the most avid and active enemies of foreignisms today are the guardians of the purity of the French language, whether in Quebec or in France per se. This concern for purity is long-standing in Francophonie ("the French-speaking world") and its linguistic tone-setters. It certainly predates the military and colonialist rivalry between France and England in both the Old World and the New. It also predates a more fleeting rivalry that may have existed on particular pre-World War I occasions (and locations) between French and German as to which of them was to be considered the primary language of "exact science" in mainland Europe and in the rest of the civilized world. Indeed, the French campaign against "foreignisms" of whatever kind may well predate the founding by royal edict of the Academy Francaise itself (1635), and the campaign certainly does not depend for either its existence or its success on any help that might be forthcoming from that August body of "immortals" that the royal edict commissioned. Indeed, it seems to derive from the very fact of rivalry with its two great and immediate neighbors, each of whom had pretensions of grandeur and power that could easily be considered worrisome by the "unfortunate" party (*"la belle France"*) trapped for all eternity between the two of them, as the processes of modernization (urbanization, industrialization, and colonization) played themselves out.

THE MESSINESS OF EVERYDAY DISCOURSE AND ITS DISCONTENTS

Purity is not easy to come by, neither in language nor in the rest of life. Indeed, real life is marked by "negative entropy", that is, natural disorder insofar as human traits and goal behavior are concerned. Of course, as some linguists never tire of telling us, "Language is different". In a well-formed (correct) sentence, words do not come in just any or random order. The "grammar" of the language dictates where the subject of a previously unuttered sentence must come in that language. And if we sometimes (or even frequently) don't follow the grammar when speaking—grammar actually being deduced from many samples of utterances, rather than existing as a separate entity in and of itself—then we are usually much more careful to be correct when writing. The arbiters of "good writing" (teachers, writers, editors, and other literary "mavens") have imposed upon the literacy acquisition process the grammatical rules that they have pieced together from samples, far and wide, of educated writing in language X and, what is more, have made us aware of these rules and of our obligation (as bearers and purveyors of literacy) to follow and foster these rules (as far as possible, particularly when speaking formally, under pain of being considered just plain messy or unlettered as far as producing well-formed sentences is concerned.

A very similar process transpires when purity is stressed by language authorities. Languages are by nature social entities, as long as their speakers are well disposed toward each other. They interact with one another, particularly with neighboring or visiting languages, and both borrow and lend words, phrases, and even sentence patterns to one another. However, the authorities of propriety in language may consider such intrusions of "foreign elements" or "influences" into language X to be undesirable, doubly so in writing and triply so in serious or educated writing. Making a population of native speakers conscious of foreignisms that should be avoided and even combated by the well-educated is tantamount to mounting a "purity campaign" for the betterment, protection, and beautification of language X. In all such purity campaigns, the enemy to be opposed is isolated and well identified, since it is rare to consider any and all borrowings equally objectionable.

The most objectionable enemy is the language of a serious opponent or rival, one that could do serious damage not only to language X per se but to the polity, culture, economy, and religion associated with it. Just as there are no two neighboring countries that never have political problems with one another, it should not surprise us that purity campaigns come and go as the underlying problems between their associated polities wax and wane, come and go. Polities that have posed longstanding and serious problems (including language problems) for each other are frequently found to engage in purity campaigns vis-à-vis borrowings from the other's language. Note, for example, the brief but intense anti-French sentiments that derived from French opposition to the United States' policy toward Iraq at the United Nations from the spring to fall of 2003. Previously innocent terms such as "French fries" and politically innocent behaviors such as purchasing French wines immediately became politically incorrect in the United States for a period of weeks. As is typical of most language planning in the United States, no one is quite sure of where this campaign began. There is still a political residue of that altercation insofar as American vacation travel to France is concerned, but the language altercation per se was never elevated to the level of a full-fledged purity campaign against French and even the brief resentment that cropped up was probably reinforced by long-harbored American tourist animosities toward the condescension of French hospitality.

SOME LONG-STANDING LANGUAGE PURITY POLICIES

Language purity efforts are examples of attempts to "clean up" messiness in the written language and to bring even educated spoken usage into greater conformity with the sharpened political differences that arise between polities and their associated cultures. Just as polities do not permit foreign powers to establish a foothold on their soil, so some languages have been struggling for generations not to permit foreign languages to establish "beachheads" in their language. Such struggles can go on for generations and are indications of the hold of history on current usage. The reluctance of Czech to the "naturalization" of Germanisms, or of Korean to the adoption of Japanese loans, or of Icelandic to grant "visitors" status to any foreignism whatsoever, or of Hebrew to officially adopt the manifold Yiddishisms of everyday speech (all of which may well predate the revernacularization of Hebrew) are all well known and are doubtlessly related to essential and longstanding aspects of the national self-consciousness and of the linguistic self-consciousness involved in each case. Curiously enough, such unwelcome guests must be recognized and rejected both quickly and effortlessly. Since mastery or even a working-familiarity with the taboo language may be uncommon, the purity-enforcing authorities my need to publish or otherwise familiarize the public with lists of proscribed words ("words to avoid", "no-no words") that should be steered clear of. Such avoidance patterns are difficult to inculcate under most circumstances (particularly in informal writing or speaking), especially when the offending language is only peripherally known and utilized. But it is particularly difficult to do so when the offending language is already marginalized to say the least, and when the two are linguistically closely related (but more about this later). Here it suffices to say that the cultivation of purity exacts a price that may frequently be an expensive one, financially, attitudinally, and cognitively all at the same time. Nevertheless, that being granted, it may still be a price that the "authorities" judge to be well worth paying.

How the Pursuit of Purity Plays Out in French Today

The two major champions of French today are France itself and its cultural offspring, Quebec Province in Canada. In this instance, the offspring has adopted a more vigorous and punitive (or intrapunitive) stance than the mother country. Both sets of authorities are governmentally institutionalized in offices, bureaus and/or councils, boards, or committees that have been appointed to oversee the pride, purity, and exclusivity of the French that is employed, not only governmentally but "out in the real world" as well. The French government offers prizes and recognition for literary works in "good French" and, at times, communicates its disfavor with those (persons or publications) judged to be utilizing less than optimally desirable French. A frequent bone of contention is in the realm of popular technology. Here, English is commonly thought to have "the edge" over French, being more looked up to and preferred in conjunction with matters technical and mechanical, even within France itself.

The brouhaha over the proper French equivalent term for the English word "fax" (the latter already being widely in use in French publications and in oral French among rather well-educated native speakers) may be considered a case in point. The originally preferred substitute term in French was *"poste electronique"*, but this soon proved to be too long and unwieldy (not to mention its utter unsuitability for use as a verb) to attract much support from the public at large. The latter were admonished by Prime Minister Dominique de Villepin to keep in mind that pomposity "is a thing of which you cannot have too much" (*National Post*, Toronto, June 15, 2005, p. 3). Accordingly, many business cards and letterheads carried the unwieldy term, instead of "fax", for a brief period in the mid-1990s when, quite suddenly, it fell from favor. I began to receive letters in which *poste electronique* was carefully crossed out on official letterheads and the word "fax" typed in instead. Once, when I asked my correspondent (an illustrious professor in France), "Since when had 'fax' become a proper French word?", I received the somewhat gruff response that "fax" had always been a French word since the English took it from the French *"facsimile"* (shades of Ataturk, see text to come). Obviously then, if true, the English were less concerned about using a French borrowing than the French were initially concerned about reclaiming it from English. This reversal of the onus of borrowing overlooks the fact that the direction of immediate borrowing may differ from the direction of historical borrowing (and, therefore, the inevitable slipperiness of all donor–borrower discussions). The aforementioned little tale also reveals how dependent the recognition of "impurity" is upon a speech community in its sensitivity to foreign markedness, a sensitivity that language planning specialists may seek to increase or decrease in accord with their own agendas. English never considered "fax" to be a foreign word because it grew full-blown out of their vaunted econotechnical know-how. French authorities finally threw in the towel on this one, finally deciding that "If you can't beat them, join them!" Accordingly, they belatedly decided that "fax" also was not a foreign word, since it was derived from the same illustrious Latin base out of which French *en toto* is derived.

Other Purity Seekers

Preserving the purity of one's "beloved language" has long played more of a role in Germany than it has in England, although an anti-French bias has shown up briefly at different times in each case. The cult of purity took hold in early modern English in the context of the "anti-inkhorn sentiments" (i.e., opposition to the heightened frequency of exaggeratedly learned neologisms, almost all of them of French origin) which characterized certain English authors and journalists of that age. A similar revolt against "putting on airs" via a superabundance of learned "Frenchisms" also arose in the mid-19th century United States. The basically Germanic nature of authentic (earliest) English was then felt to be threatened and a "Germanic English" movement (on behalf of the "American Language") sprang to the rescue (Molee, 1888). Finally, to partially even the score, a number of pro-French movements have arisen in Europe, and in one case, that of Kamal Pasha Ataturk's efforts to Europeanize (modernize) post-World War I Turkish. French loanwords were particularly preferred over all others, at the same time that Arabic (Ottoman) and Persian were rejected (Landau, 1984).

The official governmental view in the latter connection was explicitly purity related, because French itself was officially considered to be derived from Turkish ("Great Sun Theory"), introducing a Frenchism into Turkish was not tantamount to increasing the language's burden of foreignisms but, actually, the totally laudatory welcoming back into the pure Turkish fold of a long-strayed term. Also, after centuries of anti-Frenchism, tracing all the way back to Johann Gustav Herder (1744–1804) and even before, and after many decades of preferring neologisms based entirely on old Germanic roots (e.g, *"ferensprecher"* instead of "telephone", and *"ferenzeher"* instead of "television", both later replaced by "internationalisms"), German language spokespersons recently announced, that in view of the American affront to the United Nations in connection with its unilateral invasion of Iraq in 2003, the number of French borrowings into German would be increased at the expense of Americanisms, notwithstanding the worldwide currency of the latter. In other words, "Frenchisms" are not as bad as "anglicisms" insofar as their adulterating effects on German are concerned. Once more we note how the world of interpolity affairs, rather than linguistic considerations alone or even primarily, can influence a recourse to purism or to "most favored donor" status in corpus planning. The purity direction is an ever-ready way of distancing one language from another. As such, it is a particularly attractive approach to "utilize by design" whenever political considerations dictate. Language planning is a tool of national policy and the more authoritatively it is wielded, the more likely it is that it will be called upon to contribute political guidance to the directionality of corpus planning.

American and British English: The Elephants in the Language Purity Closet (since circa 1950)

The peculiar history of English has made it particularly resistant to purity efforts and, correspondingly, open to vernacularization input vis-à-vis neologisms and language planning more generally. Initially a low-

German variety, English (actually, old Anglo-Saxon) was first influenced by Celtic languages, which had preceded it across the English Channel from the mainland. Subsequently, the Roman legions made their contributions too, as did the Norseman, and, finally, as did the Normans, both when they first crossed the channel to England (1060) as well as when the now Anglo-Normans subsequently recrossed it to occupy Normandy (1144). This long and complex history of cross-linguistic warfare and population transfers made English far less monolithic than was French at the beginning of the modern era. It was also less centralized in government and less religiously homogeneous. Finally, the far briefer Roman occupation, to begin with, and the earlier and longer impact of the Reformation prior to the beginning of British settlement in the New World, both influenced the English language to modernize with a much greater and more built-in acceptance of heterodoxy in language, religion, and government than French ever experienced. English could never pretend to be the modern-day Latin, whereas French did. English did not become a bulwark of the "Church unreformed" (and, therefore, open to Latinisms), whereas French did. English was far less attracted to and less tractable for standardization and was related to the church only in that it was "a language understanded [sic!] of the people" (*Book of Common Prayer*), whereas French carried the burdens of the modern-day universal church and also inherited its universal tongue ("understanded" or not) as the primary source of borrowings and new coinage. The two very different corpus planning directions that we have been discussing in this chapter are the by-products of these two far different histories.

WHAT *CANNOT* POTENTIALLY BE AN ACCEPTABLE NEOLOGISM IN THE ENGLISH LANGUAGE?

As might have been predicted from its non-Latinate origins and its variegated and populistic composition, a single standard for English has been hard to come by, whether in ortheopy, orthography, neologism or any other linguistic orthodoxy. What French Canada has accomplished only partially and recently, a variety of its own, legitimized by local authorities and confirmed by its neighbors, English Canada, America, Australia, New Zealand, India and South Africa have accomplished earlier and more fully. The Anglo-American Empire has proven to be a tremendous importer and popularizer of words and structures that have entered the general written trove ("standard") from the local Englishes per se, and not only from the local co-territorial vernaculars. Having witnessed myself the speed with which *glitch, samizdat,* and *ciao* (coming from Yiddish, Russian, and Italian, respectively) have gained entry to the hallowed halls of the written English language (not to mention *hasta la vista baby, lumpy proletariat* or *grinch, farklem(p)t,* and *all that jazz*) I have begun to doubt that there is any natural limit at all to its potential reach and hospitality. What immigrants to the United States, the youth culture, popular mechanics, and advertising have joined together, let no person, no orthographic convention, no sense of euphony or vowel harmony, no blushing sense of propriety, whether or not accompanied by disapproving eyes rolled upward, cast asunder. The notorious English spelling does not blanch, but, instead, bellows "bring them on" to every new challenge, no matter how esoteric or unprecedented. The sky's the limit or, indeed, there is no limit at all. Such a language has no shame, no "thus far and no further". This is America! If you can imagine it, it can be said in English and in a simple and pithy English at that, even if it is neither the English of our forefathers nor of our best writers. The latter do not lack in self-confidence, but only in the ability to define themselves relative to a particular norm of "good English". They admire the advice and versatility of Churchill (see Churchill, 1908/1974).

> If an English writer cannot say what he has to say in English, and in simple English, depend upon it: it is probably not worth saying. Surely we, whose mother tongue has already won for itself such an unequaled empire over the modern world, can learn this lesson at least from the ancient Greeks. They studied their own language, they loved it, they cherished it, they adorned it, they expanded it. Surely we can learn this lesson from the ancient Greeks and bestow a little care and some proportion of the years of education to the study of a language which is perhaps to play a predominant part in the future progress of mankind. (Churchill, quoted in Fishman, 1997, pp. 206–207)

But their instincts lead them to agree even more with the view of Rupert Hughes (1920), whose position regarding neologisms is more in accord with the plebian spirit of America:

> There is such a language [as United Statish], a brilliant, growing, glowing, vivacious, elastic language for which we have [had] no spe-

cific name. Whatever we call it, let us cease to consider it a vulgar dialect of [British] English, to be used only with deprecation. Let us
study it in its splendid efflorescence, be proud of it, and true to it. Let
us put off livery, cease to be the butlers of another people's language
and try to be the masters and the creators of our own. (Hughes, 1920,
pp. 846–849)

Americans are linguistically "messier" regarding their language than
the British, who, in turn, are messier than the French. The continuum
from messy folksiness to aristocratic purity is pretty well represented by
this three-way comparison.

FOR MOST SPEAKERS (WRITERS) OF AMERICAN ENGLISH, FOLKSINESS STANDS HIGHER THAN PURITY

American English insists on being the (international) lingua franca of an
informal, egalitarian, frequently irreverent culture that places much
higher value on folksiness and trendiness than on formality and purity.
Indeed, purity has no meaning in a fusion language such as English, the
very essence of which is hybridity. Its Anglo-Saxon (and Germanic
more generally) component, its romance (French and Latin more generally) component and its "Third World" component from everywhere
else are all equally disregarded and unknown in public usage. There is
therefore no possibility of a serious and widespread purity movement in
English. It is much too late for that for a language that is so powerful at
home and abroad. It is hard to imagine what English could still gain from
a purity movement. A return to a more authentic Teutonic English of distant prior centuries is neither of interest to any prestigious authority or
"power center" within the American English or British English worlds,
nor is it within the realm of possibility either, even should friction with
the "perfidious French" continue to boil over from time to time. There
are no "politically incorrect words" derived from French that English
speakers are still trying to on an organized basis, nor did anyone believe
that the French readoption of "fax" was another coup for the "perfidious
French". Anglophonie even makes fun of itself and takes comfort from
the fact that anything that may be wrong with English stems from French
anyway. Francophonie lacks the ability to laugh at itself in the way that
Anglophonie does (see Fig. 4.1). No newspaper in France could get

Source: Dik Browne, King Features Syndicate.

FIG 4.1. Off to a Bad Start: The Initial English-French Encounter.

away with the kind of sarcasm that pervades the e-mail that I recently received from a British colleague.

ENGLISH TO BE OFFICIAL LANGUAGE OF EU

The European Commission has just announced an agreement whereby English will be the official language of the EU, rather than German which was the other possibility.

As part of the negotiations, Her Majesty's Government conceded that English spelling had some room for improvement and has accepted a five year phase-in plan that would result in what would be known as "Euro-English".

In the first year, "s" will replace the soft "c". Sertainly this will make the sivil servants jump for joy. The hard "c" will be dropped in favor of the "k". This should klear-up konfusion and keyboards kan have one less letter.

There will be growing publik enthusiasm in the sekond, when the troublesome "ph" will be replaced with "f". This will make words like "fotograf" 20% shorter.

In the 3rd year publik akseptanse of the new spelling kan be ekspekted to reach the stage where more komplikated changes are possible. Authorities will enkorage the removal of double letters, which have always ben a deterent to akurate speling. Also, al wil agre that the horible mess of the silent "e"'s in English spelling is disgrasful and that they should be don away with.

By the 4th year, peopl will be reseptiv to steps such as replasing, "th" with "z" and "w" with "v". During the fifz year, ze unesesary "o" kan be dropd from words kontaining "ou" and similar changes vud of kors be aplid to ozer kombinations of leters.

After ze fifz year, ve vil hav a reli sensible riten styl. Zer vil be no mor trubl or difikultis and evrivon vil find it ezi to understand ech ozer. Ze drem vil finali kum tru! And zen zi vorld!

CONCLUSIONS

Corpus planning continues to be very much alive in English. The fashion industry always needs new color terms, scientific nomenclature boards are active in the physical sciences and their applied branches (and even in some of the social sciences, e.g., psychology), decentralized though they be. The language's growth and change are constantly ongoing and, as with any change, it is mostly the old and rigid who oppose it (via letters to the editor). A few English teachers may be upset by the double error in "You and me are going to take him to the movies where he will sit between mother and I". However, in most instances, the lay reaction will be "What's to be so upset about?" English grammar is the way "she is spoke" and whatever she may be lacking in correctness or in purity and refinement, she more than makes up for in "folksiness" (vernacularity) and in the promise of social mobility or at least equality across social classes. Other languages have moved (or are moving) in this direction. Indeed, Pilipino was renamed Filipino in order to signal that such a move was not at all objectionable to the language's authorities at that particular time, only to be subsequently reversed. Hebrew too has become more accepting of "what they say in the marketplace" and its once highly visible and famous Academy has retired to a position of much more modest public visibility. It's major preoccupation nowadays is the preparation of a great dictionary that includes all varieties of Hebrew through the millennia (e.g., ancient Hebrew, medieval [Rabbinic] Hebrew, and current newspaper Hebrew with a good sample of adolescent slang). In general, there seems to be less discomfort in downward metaphorical shifting then there used to be, and that too is an American influence, which has worldwide corpus planning consequences. However, downward stylistic shifting in French can be mistaken for crudity and lack of education, whereas in English it signals comraderie, friendliness, shared *Gemeinshaft* and relaxed enjoyment of the moment (see Fig. 4.2).[1] Truly, vernacularity rules the English waves!

---

[1]The circular figures used throughout this book were all drawn by Avi Fishman (Sloan-Kettering International Division, NY).

REFERENCES

Churchill, W. S. (1908). The joys of writing. In *Complete speeches, 1897–1963* (Vol. 1, p. 904). New York/London: Bowker.

Hughes, R. (1920, May). Our Statish language. *Harper's Magazine*, pp. 846–849.

Landau, J. (1984). *Ataturk and the modernization of Turkey*. Leiden: E. J. Brill.

Molee, E. (1888). *Plea for an American language or Germanic English*. Chicago: Anderson.

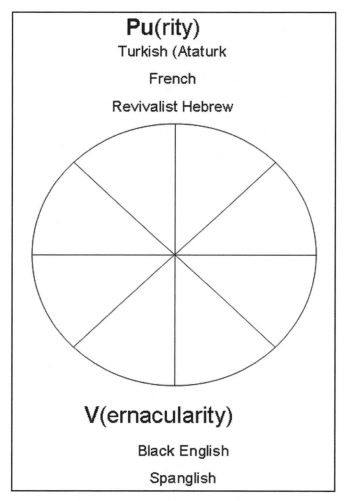

FIG. 4.2. Purity vs. Vernacularity.

5

The Bipolar Dimension of Uniqueness Versus Westernization

The bipolar dimension of corpus planning that is discussed in this chapter is not unrelated to the one we have just examined. Indeed, some might see it as an intensification of its predecessor, "purism/vernacularity", but it really functions differently enough to be treated in its own right. Superficially, purism and uniqueness may seem to be pretty much the same thing, but the pursuit of uniqueness is a much harder "row to hoe". Purism is frequently particularly opposed to a given source of borrowings, for example, English borrowings into French, Russian borrowings into Polish, or Japanese borrowings into Korean. Uniqueness, on the other hand lacks any such specific "point of avoidance" orientation. Uniqueness opposes any and all borrowings, no matter from where they may come. Supporters of uniqueness would be as much opposed to Greenlandisms as to Americanisms in searching for or evaluating a neologism for "CD Rom" or for "chocolate latte" In either case, the uniqueness of the particular beloved language would be compromised, leading, inevitably, to a similar perception of the danger of pollution for the uniqueness of the speech community itself.

IS "UNIQUENESS" REALLY POSSIBLE AT ALL?

Natural languages exist within clusters or "families" of related languages. Question: How "unique" can Gallego be (if that were to be the driving goal among its major activists) surrounded as it is by an extremely similar Portuguese, by a very similar Spanish, and by a mostly Brazilian resident Gallego diaspora? Very few of the world's 5,000+ languages are "isolates", that is, really unrelated to any other language or grouping of languages anywhere in the world. Such groupings or clusters of structurally related languages are called "language families". Of course, many more languages are perspectively unique, that is, their speakers believe that their languages are linguistic "orphans", and that no other language in the whole wide world, "regardless of what linguists say", is in any way similar to theirs. Both the Hungarian and the Finnish linguistic communities have such convictions, and, except for the recognition that they have of one another, actually call themselves "orphans in Europe" in their national and religious hymns and anthems. However, although both of them have few or no "immediate family" close at hand, they are both the current chief linguistic representatives of the Asian incursions into early medieval Europe. The Finns and Hungarians remained stranded in Europe after Ghengis Khan and his thousands of Mongol horsemen, who followed him to and through the very gates of Rome, withdrew, and left behind a genetic pool that is still evident in European DNAs to this very day. If we examine the Uighur-related languages of East Asia today (as well as several smaller languages both in Europe and in Asia), it becomes clear that neither Hungarian nor Finnish need to feel as "lonely" or as "orphaned" as their great romantic nationalist movements claimed was the case in the early 19th century, when their anthems were adopted. Once again we may note that uniqueness is much harder to attain and substantiate than to *claim*, but it is the latter (the claim) that influences corpus planning and motivates and mobilizes populations to attempt to alter their language in a particular direction.

THE PURITY AND THE UNIQUENESS WORLD VIEWS COMPARED

Uniqueness is a much more extreme and difficult goal to attain than is purity. It constitutes a rejection of any and all influences or borrowings from other languages, no matter how similar or dissimilar they may be. Purity efforts are typically aimed at particularly dynamic or powerful languages that tend to be disproportionately influential because their cultural, economic, religious and/or military might are powerful. This was true of French in much of Europe during the first half of the 19th century, of German in the second half of that same century, particularly in central and Eastern Europe, and of Chinese (Mandarin) in neighboring Korea and Vietnam during the 18th century and both earlier and even later. *Purism* has, therefore, often been identified with local patriotism or resistance against a powerful outsider and with the establishment of self-pride and the dignity of one's own culture, in language as well as in other realms of human endeavor such as art, music, customs, costumes, and even architecture. Although there may still be a reality factor that governs purism efforts to some extent, uniqueness efforts constantly face much higher hurdles and, therefore, are far more unrealistic in their grounding.

Uniqueness does not pertain to any particular foreign influence but to any and all such influences, whether from within "the family" or from without. Such total imperviousness to all interactions with outside peoples, products, and processes is generally considered unrealistic, if not retrogressive and simply impossible. If there is any faint glimmer of hope for the success of uniqueness, it lies with the few isolates. These languages, perhaps the last remaining members of what were once entire families of related languages that existed in much earlier (even prehistoric) times, are already "naturally" different from most others and unrelated to them. If this uniqueness direction of development can be continued under language planning auspices for modernization purposes, then its goal need not be a will-o'-the-wisp. But it remains a big "if", nevertheless, and will ultimately be dependent on the intensity and durability of the interactions of the carriers of putative uniqueness with the world's major suppliers of modern ideas and artifacts.

HOW DID/DOES BASQUE DO IT (OR DOES/DID IT)?

Basque is, apparently, the major isolate in Europe today. We no longer know for sure what ingredients from prior or contemporary languages went into its creation, although there seems to have been some long-term contact with Celtic varieties now still extant and known as Breton, Irish Gaelic, Welsh, Scottish Gaelic (pronounced "Golic" [rhymes with "frolic"]), Manx, and Cornish. The Basque "country" was never fully conquered or occupied by the Romans, Visigoths, Moslems or even the Inquisition, until the Fascist Dictator, Francisco Franco (1892–1975), vindictively used bombers and tanks against their comparatively primitive defenses in mountain and coastal strongholds. Upon his death, the newly reestablished Spanish Republic (1978) granted the Basque region autonomy and placed its language on a par with Spanish within that territory (1979). The autonomous Basque community (see Fig. 5.1) was immediately faced with two gigantic tasks: (1) modernization of their ancient tongue so that it and its speakers could function effectively in the modern world, and (2) win over to this language the nearly 80% of Basques (not to mention the 100% of outsiders who have sought work in the vast Basque iron and steel industries and remained there for the long-term) who had long forgotten any Basque that their grandparents may once have known, or who never knew any Basque to begin with (immigrating from areas in which it was totally unknown). Because Basque monolinguals were almost nonexistent by the time of Franco's demise (except in isolated rural valleys from which the urbanized immigrants steered away), several Hispanicisms had been popularly adopted into the home and neighborhood Basque discourse of those who still retained a working knowledge of the old and "strange" tongue.

A massive effort was undertaken by the Basque Departments of Education and the Mass Media, under the guidance of a plan proposed by the provincial government's secretariat of language policy, to improve the Basque of those who still semi-spoke it, and to render them Basque literate as well. On the other hand, non-Basque speakers were enrolled in a massive effort to "Basquecize" them via child or adult courses and out-of-class activities. Participation in these activities yielded certification at various levels of competence, entitling their bearers to qualify for promotions, raises, job tenure and other perquisites of success in the workplace. These language-acquisition efforts then made more acute than ever before the modernization of all aspects of the language (now to be used in industry, government agencies, the mass-media and even university courses).

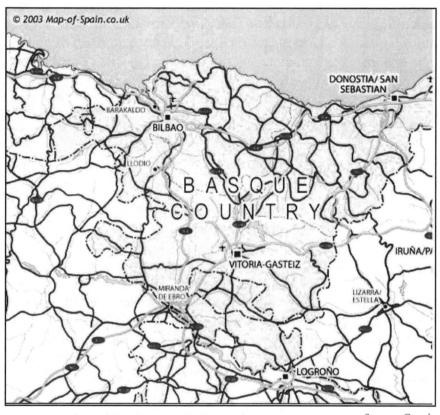

FIG. 5.1.   The Autonomous Basque Community.

Certainly such a massive effort required prior decisions and guide-
lines as to what the "new Basque" should be like with respect to such
fundamental matters as dialectal base and the orthography, new lexi-
cons, and grammatical rules that it required. Remember, that by then,
the late 1970s, all Basques of post-childhood age also spoke, read, and
wrote Spanish. The increasing Hispanicization of Basque might have
been a popular decision with the Madrid regime; it would also have
made the acquisition of Basque far easier, particularly for adults whose
language acquisition skills were clearly already quite far beyond their
prime. A paragraph from a recent bilingual publication (see Fig. 5.2)
will reveal the extent of the "uniqueness" road that was followed.

> *Q.*   *For the entire class*: From your knowledge of any and all other
> languages, how much of the following news-item can you under-
> stand?   (From *Azmosta Jakitez*, 2004, no. 48, p. 4)

THE ROLE OF COMPROMISE
IN THE PURSUIT OF UNIQUENESS

A frequently encountered problem in all literacy planning for a primarily "nonreading" X population is the selection of the dialectical base of
the literary variety. The standard variety constitutes the ordinary citi-
zen's major encounter with either formal or other than face-to-face language, for example, in schools, mass media, governmental
administrative operations, and religion. It also comes to be the variety
most impacted by speaking pronunciations among members of educated
and polite society. In the Basque case, such a choice required a painful
compromise between the most widely spoken regional dialect (in and
around Bilbao) and the most widely read and written one among the already literate public (that of San Sebastian and its environs). The latter
was selected, thereby adding yet another prop for uniqueness, since it
was also the one least influenced by foreign contacts. However, from the
very outset, one noticeable exception was made pertaining to texts for
the beginning grades. The latter received a special dispensation, permit-
ting them to be printed in the local dialect, under the assumption that this
would lessen the opposition from a major segment of the reading public

Literatura eta harrilkoa

ERREA, Inma
Iruña: Pamiela, 2003

Emakumearen zeregina literaturan eta emakume literaturaren definizio bera ere dira liburu honetan uki- turiko gaiak, eguneroko egoera batean oinarri harturik. Brigita protagonistak, bere etxeko suk- aldean garbitzen ari den bitar- tean, kultura emanaldi bat entzuten du irratian. Irratsaio horrek emakumearen eta letren arteko harremanak ikertzera bultzatzen du. Literatura arrosa, emakume literatura da? Zergatik idazle gehiago dira gizkonezkoen artean emakumezkoen artean baino? Emakume literatura, emakumeari buruzkoa edo emakumeak idatzirikoa ote da? Nork adieraziko du emakume batek baino hobeto amatasuna bezalako esperientzia bat? Horiek eta beste hainbat alderdi lantzen ditu Inma Erreak bere lanean era atsegin eta zorrotzean.

FIG. 5.2. From a Basque journal.

that might otherwise have become alienated. Language decisions are political decisions and it should not surprise us that "compromises" are frequently attempted and arrived at among disagreeing "defenders of the beloved language" themselves.

Estonian and the *Ex Nihilo* Approach to Uniqueness

Estonian is not a real orphan in Europe but a member of the small Baltoslavic language family which, today, includes Lithuanian and Latvian as well. Up until the beginning of the 20th century, Estonian was a language of rural life among peasants. After the turn of the century, both urban areas in general and the nationalist movement for political liberation from Czarist Russia in particular, grew rapidly and the need for a standard Estonian that could be fully developed to the level necessary for participation in modern European culture was becoming widely recognized. One of the linguists and nationalists who contributed substantially to such development was Johannes Aavik (1880–1973) who used an *ex nihilo* ("out of nothing") method in creating new Estonian words from randomly constituted nonsense syllables. This, of course, is the height of uniqueness (provided that "words" [combinations of randomly selected letters] that are accidentally like or reminiscent of words in other languages are set aside), since it discards family-tree affiliations, neighboring language influences, or world-language influences as sources for neologism formation from the very outset.

This proved to be a very controversial approach to lexical elaboration for the purposes of sociocultural modernization and has rarely if ever been repeated elsewhere. This method was not a total dud however, it's rejection not being an outgrowth of any negative experiences with it. Indeed, Aavik managed to gain wide support among high-school and university students as well as among young poets and writers (see Fig. 5.3 and Fig. 5.4). Perhaps the young are more inclined toward unprecedented solutions, or are more capable of accepting them. The opposition to Aavik pointed to the ahistoricity of his approach, which cuts the language's neologisms off from all of its formative roots and regularities and starts its lexical innovations from zero all over again, as if it were a totally artificial medium with no history

Two contrasting practitioners of Estonian Corpus planning: Aavik and Veski

FIG. 5.3.   Johannes Aavik.

Source: Sprachreform (Istvan Fodor
and Claude Hegege, eds. Hamburg,
Buske, 1985, v. 2, p. 311

FIG. 5.4.   J. V. Veski.

Source: Estonian Encyclopedia.
Talin, EE, p. 395 (n.d.).

whatsoever. As a result, only about 40 of the *ex nihilo* terms created by Aavik and about 15 more suggested by others took hold and have remained in the language to this very day (Ross, 1938). However, these are very small numbers, particularly when compared with the number of new terms created by Aavik's contemporary and chief rival, Johannes Veski (1873–1968), who sponsored some 160,000 new words and still could not keep up with the lexical needs of a rapidly growing, modern, and technologically oriented society. Later, Aavik departed from his original preference for *ex nihilo* creations alone and also coined neologisms using French, German, Latin, and English roots, but by then his "race" to serve as the major contributor to what the Estonian language is today had already been lost. Veski's (1912) nomenclatures were not only more plentiful but they also drew on many more sources (including many that were originally taboo for Aavik, who was, after all, something of a purist too), namely Estonia's more advanced neighbors, particularly Finnish and Russian.

In the Estonian case, we clearly see the differing status preferences of the two opposite ends of the uniqueness–internationalism dimension in operation, with respect to the lexical elaboration aspect of corpus planning and the societal consequences thereof. Aavik's *ex-nihilo* approach signals a maximal detachment from the outer world and the influences that large and powerful languages necessarily have on the small and weak ones that live in their shadow. However, Olympian detachment is not a luxury that small, weak, and unWesternized languages can really afford. They must agree to go along with modernization at least part of the way, knowing full well that there will be a disturbing price to pay, regardless of the choices that they make or the policies that they follow. Language planning alone will not fully solve this problem, but it may ameliorate it by establishing a principle that recognizes the need to control or shape any solution. The young fin de siècle (19th century) Estonian activists put it this way: "Let us be Estonians, but let us also become Europeans!" Corpus planning guided by such a principle may well slide up and down on the uniqueness–westernization dimension, depending on the need and the spirit of the times, but it must attempt not to let either end of the scale "get out of hand".

Westernization: The Other End of the Bipolar Dimension

But there are also many corpus planning occasions when the very opposite of uniqueness, namely Westernization, is exactly what the language authorities feel that they must seek to maximize. A commonly recognized hidden agenda in just such an approach to the modernization of a local language is to give its users an advantage in connection with acquiring English (or whatever the regionally dominant language of international trade may be, e. g., Mandarin/Putinghua, Hindi, Malay, etc.). The importance of English in all sorts of higher (post-elementary) education makes it appear to be an "open sesame" in many parts of the world. Parents and pupils alike are often mesmerized by its pursuit for years before its formal introduction begins. Due to the chronic lack of sufficient (and of sufficiently proficient) English teachers, Westernization as a guiding principle for national language modernization is one way in which to appear to bridge the gap. It is "a two for the price of one" solution, which appears to many to have much to be said for it. It promises both "freedom from the oppressor" (the former colonial powers of the West) as well as greater linguistic proximity to English. It is one way in which the modernist demotion of the national language can be kept from becoming an open, public issue, provided English per se does not appear to come under Anglophone auspices.

Many developing languages throughout the world have espoused societal modernization through Westernization via English at one time or another, and many others have given in to this process, whether they genuinely wanted to or not. To fight it would have meant to oppose a dream of the people, to set roadblocks to social mobility for the poor, who can afford no other means of accessing English, and whose high school-dropout rate might indirectly benefit from an approach that can also be touted as more English friendly at the same time. "Westernisms", after all, are not necessarily anglicisms and what's good for the goose (e.g., French, in the case of "fax") is also good for the gander (e.g., Turkish).

English itself has not been immune to a related approach in earlier centuries, when French was the language of progress and of "international" emulation, at least throughout much of Europe. Subsequently,

German influences displaced the bulk of earlier French ones and succeeded briefly in becoming the universal language of science and technology, particularly throughout Central and Eastern Europe. Germany's defeat in two world wars and its association with the hated Nazi regime (*Der todt ist ein Meister aus Deutchland* [Death is a master workman from Germany] in Paul Celan's (2004) unforgettable words, ruined its chances of widespread acceptance as a major basis of corpus expansion for newly modernizing languages, but by then the obviously greater utility of English had probably already turned the latter into the prime model of modernization almost everywhere. French, German and Russian now need to be studied by speakers of even smaller languages in their respective orbits for their own sakes (e.g., reading Voltaire, Herder, and Trotsky in the languages in which they wrote), rather than as languages of wider communication with unexpected ancillary fringe advantages (see Fig. 5.5).

Russian and Pilipino

Russian has had to defend itself twice in the process of the modernization of its national language. Until late in the 18th century (and even later than that in the case of some writers), Russian Old Church Slavonic was the language of learning and of the written record. Its relationship to modern Russian was roughly of the order of Latin's relationship to modern French at around that time, except that almost no one was writing Latin novels or publishing Latin journals in France by then. The difference between the spoken and the written language in Russia was no great problem for the wealthy and educated, who could afford the additional time necessary in order to read and write on secular topics in what was essentially a "religious classical". However, the absence of public education essentially cut off the urban lower class and the entire peasantry from literacy, but this was considered by writers and other language authorities to be a moderate price to pay for maintaining the "ancient, authentic and glorious language of Mother Russia".

Other Eastern Orthodox cultures (e.g., Serbian, Bulgarian, Ukrainian, or Macedonian) also faced the same problem, and each of them engaged in authoritative language planning in order to finally bring to the fore the solution of "write as you speak", to quote, once again, Vuk

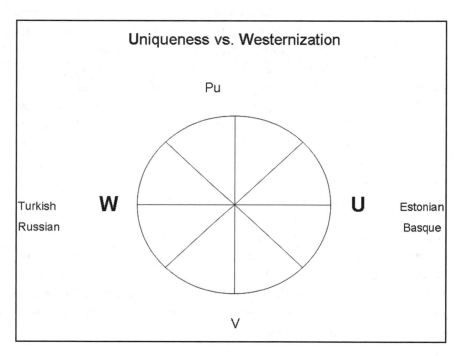

FIG. 5.5. Uniqueness Versus Westernization.

Stefanovič Karadzić (1787–1864), the great Serbian linguist and folklor-
ist, who was unconsciously paraphrasing Antonio Nebrija's comment
about writing Spanish "just the way I speak it", some 300 years earlier,
when overcoming excessive Latinization was a problem for educated
people in Spain).

One of the main reasons why many folk intellectuals (like high-
school teachers, preachers, journalists, and writers) were loathe to make
what may seem to us to be an obviously well-merited literacy-fostering
switch, was that the spoken language was suffused with foreign loan
words and even grammatical influences. Russian has remained rather
hospitable to such influences up until this very day, and not only in connection with the realms of science and technology but in the language of
everyday life as well. Since most cultured, refined, and exquisite things
came from the West (particularly from France and from Germany
throughout the 19th century and from England and, finally, America in
the 20th century), words and expressions from such points of origin
were eagerly adopted (Rogger, 1960). With the collapse of Commu-
nism, the floodgates were opened to an influx of Americanisms, which
still marks both colloquial and "literary"(standard) Russian today. It is
the acceptance of such internationalisms (in most cases, Americanisms)
for school and governmental spoken and written use that pinpoints their
acceptability by authoritative corpus planning bodies. Although com-
plaints about "too many" and "too fast" changes are still voiced from
time to time, they are merely isolated cases of foot-dragging in the face
of a widely accepted and historically deep trend which runs quite
counter to that of uniqueness.

Filipino-Pilipino-Filipino

In the 1960's the unifying national language of the Philippines was
called "Pilipino" (despite the fact that the language does not commonly
permit a word initial "p"); today it is called "Filipino". And thereby (the
replacement of a word initial "p" by a word initial "f") hangs a corpus
planning tale. Throughout their struggle for independence from the
United States, the leaders of the Philippines bemoaned the absence of a
widely known supraregional variety or language that could serve to tie
all of its disparate and far-flung peoples and cultures into a new, dy-

namic, and harmonious whole. It was not that such an indigenous variety simply didn't exist. There was one such variety and it functioned for both the nationwide spread of trade and ideas. It was Tagalog, the vernacular of the Manila region and surrounding areas. The centrality of that variety for inter-island government and trade and its acceptance for both written and spoken interregional communication made it an obvious candidate for the role of national language, but it was long feared by those who led the independence movements (first against Spain, then against the United States, then against Japan and, finally, against the United States again) that the other far-flung regions (and regional languages) would object to the elevation of Tagalog over the others.

Finally, because it was obviously the most widely known and used of all the Philippine local languages (as well as being the vernacular of the capitol itself), Tagalog was chosen for the coveted role of national language. However, in order to obviate possible interethnic rivalry, the central governmental variety was initially renamed Filipino (1959). Filipino was essentially Tagalog, a language already widely used in all of the islands for interisland trade and other commercial purposes (not unlike the use of Bazaar Malay in Indonesia [later renamed Indonesian]), but with one potentially important difference: its advocates specified that it was to be "enriched" by also drawing upon the "genius" of the other major indigenous languages of the Philippines. This would not only appeal to local pride outside of Manila, but it would help counteract the vestiges of linguistic colonialism by ruling out the many Americanisms and Hispanicisms with which the language of the Capital was popularly associated. A language academy was established in order to expand Filipino so that it could cope with all of the functions of a modern (or modernity seeking) supralocal national culture. However, in the seeds of its uniqueness-oriented birth, there also lay the seeds of its ultimate decline and replacement.

The guided process of enrichment of the written governmental variety, Filipino, proceeded much more slowly than the spontaneous unplanned process of the addition of English calques, translation loans and out-and-out borrowings in everyday Metropolitan (Manilan) speech. Because the degree to which English actually entered into anyone's informal usage, both written and spoken, was social class and education-related and distance from Manila related, pressure began to mount (po-

litically motivated, to be sure) to legitimize the popular usage of the un-
derprivileged, instead of opposing it. This could be done by implicitly
and explicitly recognizing and dignifying a variety that was closer to
that employed by the masses themselves, insofar as acceptance of English influences were concerned. Accordingly, a new variety called Filipino was recognized in 1973 to become the new national language. It too
was conceptualized as a language uniquely incorporating elements from
all other Philippine languages, but now these would also include the major foreign languages used in the Philippines (*de facto*: English Spanish
and the Manila *lingua franca*). Thus, instead of aiming at "uniqueness"
via a compromise variety developed out of the disparate indigenous languages of the country, the authorities moved quietly, without fanfare, in
the direction of Westernization and internationalization. They have de-
fended this change, not only on populist and democratic grounds, but
also on the grounds of spreading familiarity with English and Spanish,
two international languages that have long been associated with the
country (therefore, "not all that foreign", after all) and which can serve it
well in commerce and tourism in the future. The latter consideration
may actually become a growing trend throughout the world, particularly
in former British and American colonies and spheres of influence,
whose political independence was also gained in the late 1940s and during the 1950s (Fishman, Conrad, & Rubal-Lopez, 1996).[1] However, the
continued symbolic commitment to also sampling the "genius" of all local languages (indigenous or not) remains a uniquely Philippine stress
within the former colonial nations.

Malacanag

Manila

WHEREAS the 1987 Constitution provides that the "national language
of the Philippines is Filipino"; that "as it evolves it shall be further developed and enriched on the basis of the existing Philippine and other
languages"; and that for "purposes of communication and instruction
the official languages of the Philippines are Filipino and, until otherwise provided by law, English", and

---

[1]Note particularly the chapter on the Philippines, op. cit.

WHEREAS the intensified use of Filipino language in official transactions, communications and correspondence in governmental offices will hasten greater understanding and appreciation among the people of governmental programs, projects and activities throughout the country, thereby serving as an instrument of unity and peace for national progress,

NOW, THEREFORE, I, CORAZON C. AQUINO, President of the Philippines, do hereby enjoin all departments/bureaus/offices/ [and] instrumentalities of government to undertake the following:

1. Take steps to enhance the use of Filipino in all official transactions and correspondence in their respective offices, whether national or local.

2. Assign one or more personnel, as may be necessary, in every office, to take charge of all communications and correspondence.... in Filipino.

3. Translate into Filipino the names of offices, buildings, public edifices, divisions or instrumentalities, and, if so desired, imprint below, in smaller letters, the English text.

4. Filipinize the "Oath of Office" for governmental officials and personnel.

5. Make as part of the training program for personnel development in each office proficiency in the use of Filipino in official communications and correspondence.

DONE in the City of Manila, this 25th day of August, in the year of Our Lord nineteen hundred eighty-eight.

(Department of Education, Culture and Sports and Institute of Philippine Languages, 1991, pp. 11–12).

THE LANGUAGE PLANNING ROLE OF LOCAL HISTORY AND POLITICS

The initial direction of Philippine corpus planning, while not exactly in the direction of "uniqueness" (see below for "Sprachbund oriented corpus planning"), would have left Pilipino more closely related to the other modernizing Austronesian languages (e.g., the state languages of

Indonesia and Malaysia), a very unique set of languages on the world scene, and, accordingly, less related to the European languages that had played such a significant role in the Philippine's own history and were destined to remain significant in the entire region's foreseeable future. The "Filipino" solution was a classical political compromise. While the Austronesian nature of the language remained eminently clear, the potential for gaining a head start for students of English, young and old, was too promising to shrug off. The leadership remained satisfied that it had successfully opted for more than a little of both uniqueness and Westernization, a view with which the lay public does not seem to have any quarrel.

THE DILEMMAS OF GREAT LANGUAGES

A similar problem faces several former Soviet republics today, as they face the distinctly different blandishments of Russian and of English as potential influences in their corpus planning. For example, many Turkic languages today are vacillating between these two routes to modernization and internationalization. But since Russian too has absorbed many Americanisms, some Americanisms have found their way into Uzbek via the "back door", so to speak, "biznesmen", "internet" and "computer" being good representatives of this process. The Russian influences undoubtedly have a head start (going back to Czarist days), and are valuable for trade and security arrangements with the other newly independent Central Asian "stan" republics (Kazakhstan, Kyrgyzstan, Tajikistan, Turkmenistan, Uzbekistan, etc.), but it has also been traditionally resisted as well and, therefore, Russian retains many of its formerly negative pre- "overtones". English, on the other hand, comes bearing capitalism, democracy, youth, culture, and modern technology and without the onus of centuries of occupation and anti-Uzbek policies such as those that Russian can't shake off. Under such circumstances, a "bird in the hand" will very probably not be precipitously abandoned, during the time that direct contact with Americanisms slowly increases. The "smart money" is on the latter as constituting the road to true Westernization. This two-pronged and two-staged reality is also faced by many other corpus planning establishments that labor in the penumbra of a regional great power's (indeed, often a former colonial taskmaster's) language of wider communication, in addition to that of the colossus that stalks the world. Most recently, China too has become a purveyor of Westernisms, both for its own minorities and for those in neighboring countries that have historically been exposed to Chinese cultural, commercial, and/or military influences.

PURITY OF CHINESE LANGUAGE DEBATED
by Xung Zhigang
China Daily (Singapore), September 13, 2004, p. 1

Few people living in large Chinese cities like Bejing and Shanghai are still unfamiliar with loan words in their daily lives such as *maidanglao* (McDonalds), *kendeji* (KFC) and *xingbake* (Starbucks). Meanwhile, technical terms taken from other languages, especially English, are even more common. They include *nami* (nanometer) or *yinqing* (engine), to name just a few. In fact, the emergence of loan words in Chinese has been so fast that official statistics suggest about 1,000 such new words are added to the Chinese vocabulary each year. Some Chinese linguists hail the practice as a symbol of vitality and openness of the Chinese language, with a history of more than 5,000 years. They say the mushrooming of foreign loan words in Chinese is an inevitable trend, given China's closer exchanges with the outside world and the speed-up in its globalization bid.

Nowadays, it has become almost a fashion for young people to speak their native language mingled with a few English words, to show either their educational background or just for fun. Even the official Chinese-language newspapers are flush with English abbreviations such as WTO (World Trade Organization), CBD (central business district), GDP (gross domestic product), and CEO (chief executive officer). However, the use of Chinese mixed with English words has triggered hot debates among amid pundits and linguists about how to safeguard the uniqueness of Chinese while keeping its openness and fostering valuable international contacts.

Media commentator, Xue Yong, justifies the use of English words as a move to enrich Chinese words and strengthen their creativity. Likewise, Xue stresses that the acceptance of foreign words in Chinese should be taken as a necessary linguistic strategy to embrace new things. Dong Kun, deputy director of the Institute of Language Studies under the Chinese Academy of Social Sciences, goes further to point out that the increasing use of foreign words in Chinese is a new direction for the Chinese language to evolve.

His judgment has been well supported by the compilation of English words commonly used by the Chinese in a special part of the newly edited *Modern Chinese Dictionary*, the country's most authoritative guidebook for the use of standard Chinese. Included in the dictionary are CD, VCD and CT (computer tomography), often called CAT scans.

The endorsement, however, has been criticized as "inappropriate" by others who warn that tolerating the nonstandard use of English words in Chinese will erode the language and even endanger its existence. Liu Bin, former Minister of Education, believes that standardizing the use of new words is the basic and most important task for any language in the world. "Allowing disorder to exist will greatly undermine the healthy development of our mother language", he notes. Liu is now a member of the Standing Committee of the National People's Congress, the country's top legislature, and also a member of its Education, Science, Culture and Public Health Committee. He underlines the "alarming" and "abusive" use of English in Chinese language newspapers and magazines, saying it violates Article 11 of the National Language Law of the People's Republic of China (enacted in 2001). "Chinese is strong enough to ensure that any English word and abbreviation can be given an accurate Chinese translation", he argues, rather than using the English words themselves.

The aforementioned citation has been brought, notwithstanding its length, to illustrate the diversity of corpus planning rationales and opinions that are manifested by the language authorities even in authoritarian societies. The outside world may be both pursued and rejected. Were this not the case, it would be far easier to adopt a consistent and unchanging policy. Sometimes diametrically opposing views are pursued simultaneously when authorities are confronted by philosophically and practically conflicting options. Neither choice is without some negative consequences, but both are to some extent, also desirable and desired at the same time. That is why corpus planning frequently entails oscillations and changes of direction, particularly so when (but not only when) the past is associated with a unique greatness that cannot be simply set aside to pursue the blandishments of modernity and globalization.

Of course, there are other than language-related issues that divide the authorities in any sociocultural setting. That is why corpus planning decisions are so likely to be reversed. It is necessary to see them as part and parcel of the political and politicized rivalries and antagonisms that exist in all human society. When the directional differences in corpus planning fall together with other directionally conflicted concerns (political. religious, economic, etc.), the result may easily be interpreted as an instance of "language conflict". However, very little (if any) language conflict is ever really about language per se, and even less is about language alone. If one looks a little deeper, below the surface of language-related rhetoric, one usually finds other societal fissures with which the corpus planning differences co-occur. When that is the case, language, being so symbolic of culture-group membership as a whole, may be easily and falsely blamed for the contentiousness in society more generally. Language is rarely the only or chief culprit in so called "language conflict", whether or not the uniqueness goal is advanced, or the internationalization goal is pursued in corpus planning. This is also why, as much of the world moves ever further along the path of globalization, the historical and still emotional tug of uniqueness will probably never disappear entirely and, by its very presence, serve to temper and restrain globalization in various degrees.

REFERENCES AND FURTHER READINGS

Celan, P. (2004). *Todesfuge und andere Gedichte*. Suhrkamp, Frankfurt A. M.

Cruz, I. (1991). A nation searching for a language finds a language searching for a name. *English Today, 7*, 17–21.

Department of Education, Culture and Sports and Institute of Philippine Languages. (1991). *Primer on executive order no. 335*. Manila: Philippine Information Agency.

Fishman, J. A., Conrad, A., & Rubal-Lopez, A. (Eds.). (1996). *Post-imperial English: Status change in former British and American colonies, 1940–1990*. Berlin: Mouton de Gruyter.

Gonzalez, A. (1980). *Language and nationalism: The Philippine experience thus far*. Quezon City: Ateneo de Manila University Press.

Helgi, V., & Ribenis, K. (2000). *Johannes Aavik and Estonian lunguage Innovation: Bibliography, 1901–1996*. Tallinn: Akadeemia Truk.

Llamzon, T. (1996). A requiem for Pilipino, In B. P. Sibayan & A. Gonzalez (Eds.), *Language planning and the building of a national language: Essays in honor of Santiago A. Finacier on his 92nd birthday* (pp. 315–323). Manila: University of the Philippines and Philippine Normal College.

McFarland, C. (1998). English enrichment of Filipino. *Philippine Journal of Linguistics, 29,* 73–90.

Rozniak, Z. (1988). Bilingualism and bureaucratism. *Nationalities Papers, 16*(2), 260–271.

Rogger, H. (1960). *National consciousness in eighteenth-century Russia.* Cambridge: Harvard University Press.

Ross, A. S. (1938). Artificial words in present-day Estonian. *Transactions of the Philological Society, London,* 64–72.

Veski, J. V. (1912). *Eesti Kitjakeele reelid.* Tallim, no publisher listed.

Wines, M. (2002, April 18). Russia resists plans to tweak the mother tongue. *New York Times,* lgpolicy-list@ccat.sas.upenn.edu

Zhigang, X. (2004, September 13). Purity of Chinese language debated. *China Daily.*

6

The Classicization Versus "Panification" Bipolar Dimension

Many of the world's most frequently spoken languages have only appeared on the scene comparatively recently, that is, in historical rather than in prehistorical times. English is actually one of the most-"Johnny-come-lately" languages on the European language scene. Although it is impossible to really date the birth of any language to a given day, month, and year, many can be roughly dated by reference to specific major events (migrations, invasions, conquests, etc.) implicated in their creation. English can be dated somewhat more precisely than most because we know roughly when the Angels, Saxons, and Jutes crossed the channel from their coastal area in the Low Countries and landed in England. This occurred shortly after the Roman legions, who had succeeded in incorporating the southern part of what is now England into the Roman Empire, were withdrawn to serve elsewhere because the heartland of the Empire itself was being invaded from the then Germanic east. The massive arrival of fierce Germanic warriors throughout central Europe may also have been responsible for the further movement of the Angels, Saxons, and Jutes across the Channel and the consolidation of English there when these tribes united relatively "soon" thereafter.

The Romance languages began with the conquest of Gaul (France) and Iberia by Roman legions much earlier than their occupation of parts of England. Their predecessor languages were probably largely Celtic in nature, and French ultimately was constituted from such pre-Latin formations on which the vulgar Latin of various periods was superimposed (as new legions arrived and old ones were withdrawn). Plus there was some contribution from the Germanic Franks, who ultimately routed the last legions, became Christians, and slowly became the rulers of the country whose unification went on for centuries thereafter. It is difficult to decide on an approximate date for the birth of French because each of the aforementioned successive strata was centuries removed from its predecessors. Any age approximation would have to be tentative, but, whichever age is selected (ideologically preferred), it can be anchored relative to certain dates of an historically established nature.

But we have no such historically related markers to enable us to even approximate the birth of Athenian Greek (now usually referred to as Classical Greek), Hebrew, Latin , Old Church Slavonic or Sanskrit, Classical Tamil, Classical Chinese (Mandarin) nor Classical Arabic. Most of the foregoing languages are "really old", that is, older than any of the currently spoken languages of Europe (perhaps with the exception of Basque) and their exact dating is, therefore, doubly difficult and questionable. However, because of their long association with the major world religions, the already-named eight classical languages (and just a few others scattered around the globe) have lent high prestige, not only to the modern varieties associated with or derived from them, but have provided us with the very concept of *antiquity* as a widely desired language characteristic. Most people may have no exact idea of the vintage of their vernacular, but they would like it to be as old as possible. Older languages serve as models to younger ones and have adopted myths to "support" their claims. Since their "creation" is unknown or unknowable, their componentiality (in terms of prior languages that had influenced or were absorbed into them) is largely unknown and unknowable. This quasieternal backward reach and their religious associations give the Classicals an aura of purity that is probably greatly exaggerated. The upshot of all of the foregoing is that age in general and sanctified classicism in particular are characteristics that can be used or built upon by today's language planners in order to modernize and gain sociocultural support for the languages being championed. We briefly discuss two such examples of "Classicism for the purposes of modernization" Hindi (vis-à-vis Sanscrit), and Israeli (vis-à-vis Classical Hebrew).

Sanskrit

The modern movements to "revive" or revernacularize Sanscrit and to free Mother India from bondage to Britain are largely contemporaneous. No wonder then that in the search for a Hinduism-friendly vernacular to unify most of those Hindus who struggled for Indian freedom from the Christian West, Hindi (originally called Hindustani) emerged victorious, although this was neither inevitable nor easy. Gandhi favored it, as did his All India Union Party (see Fig. 6.1), even more so than they favored English or even Sanscrit itself. However much it was venerated, Sanscrit had several strikes against it: It was too Hinduism-related (and, therefore, unacceptable to Moslems, even though Gandhi supported Hindi vigorously precisely because of its linguistic proximity to Urdu (see Fig. 6.2), the most widely utilized Moslem vernacular). As a result, there was no chance that either could be serviceable for the purposes of healing the profound and volatile religious rift. Even Hindi was somewhat problematic for ordinary Hindus, since its modernization was solidly based upon Sanscrit borrowings and Sanscrit roots that only the very learned and very pious could be expected to easily understand. Even Nehru, who campaigned for the Union Party before crucial elections and who exerted quite a bit of skill and effort so as to be understood by the untutored masses, constantly complained, that when his talks were edited for rebroadcasting to audiences who had been at work, or away from their radios, or even from the their villages where his talks had originally been broadcasted "live", that his statements were so Sanscritized on rebroadcast as to be incomprehensible even to himself, the author of the remarks being presented!

THE HINDI LANGUAGE PLANNERS LAMENT

The translators and editors whom Nehru excoriated were not by any means trying to sabotage the Union Party's election campaigns. From

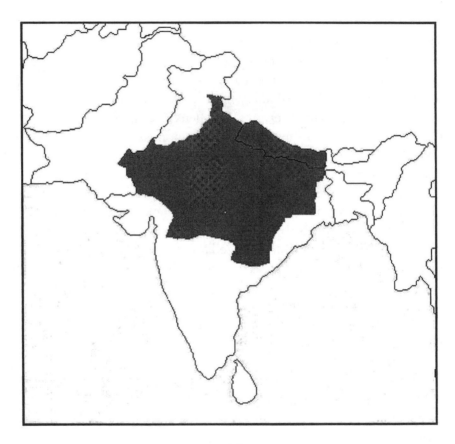

FIG. 6.1. Hindi language map.

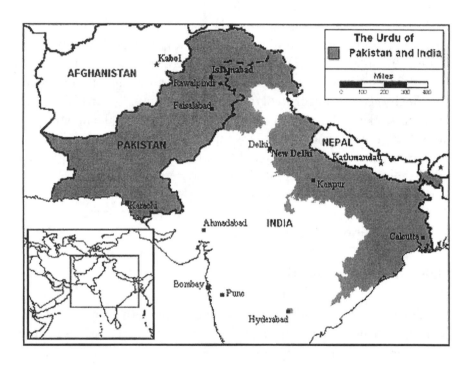

FIG. 6.2.   Urdu in Northeast India and in Pakistan.
Note: There are areas of overlap between Fig. 6.1 and Fig. 6.2, i.e.,
areas in which both languages are widely claimed to be spoken. It is
difficult to draw non-controversial language maps.

their point of view, they were merely trying to present Hindi at its most distinguished, educated, upper-class level. Ordinary Hindus might be mystified by a recondite Sanscrit word (or root) substituted for a plain Hindi word here and there, but they could easily ask others whom had received more education what that word meant. They would be building up their Hindi thereby, leaving the Moslem listeners to be the only ones in the dark (which didn't bother the aforementioned language planners either). A real Classical past, one which the entire civilized and modernized world values (and even envies), is not easily put aside during language planning for modernization purposes. It is too important a resource in order that its fairly limitless extravernacular features (lexical inexhaustibility, orthographic standardization, and grammatical complexity) be kept out of sight (much less out of mind), particularly for the sophisticates who are constantly in awe of English (the language of the former colonizer) but, yet, are far from being unaware of the far greater virtues that the incomparably older Sanscrit has to offer to the dignity, authenticity, and creativity of modern India. Without Sanscrit, Hindi was just another of India's innumerable vernaculars; with the help of Sanscrit, it was on the way to unifying India and becoming one of the great languages of the modern world as well!

Other Classical Quandaries

In many ways, the use of Classical Arabic for modern vernacular functions in the Moslem world presents the same difficulties as does the use of Sanscrit in the Hindu sphere. Actually, in some ways, the Arabic problem is the more difficult of the two because there isn't a many-hundred-years-old vernacular literature in any of the several varieties of spoken Arabic (e.g., Egyptian, Syrian, Saudi Arabian, Iraqi, etc.), whereas all of the major spoken offspring of Sanscrit became vehicles of folk literature and religious education hundreds of years ago or more. Thus, the major varieties of current Indian vernaculars have "worked through" a *modus vivendi* with Sanscrit and must now achieve the same vis-à-vis Hindi, the rather young official language that is also, as are they, of Sanscrit origin. Indeed, the problems that exist in India are not so much vis-à-vis the manifold provincial vernaculars, but, primarily

Hindi itself. Actually, Hindi faces a "two front war", one regarding the amount of Sanscrit to incorporate for the purpose of its own embellishment and enrichment, on one hand, and, simultaneously, how different from Urdu it should become via this same Sanscritization, on the other hand. We attend to the first "front" in the present chapter and to the second "front", in chapter 7 (on Ausbau languages).

"A Little Bit of Sugar"

Urdu is the national language of Pakistan, India's neighbor to the northwest, a neighbor born out of secession from India proper. It is an ancient language of literature and poetry, but the virtual identity of informally spoken Hindi and Urdu among the unschooled majority of both populations detracts from the capacity of each of them to fully become the unmistakenly national instruments and symbols of two separate and often contentious countries. Clearly, the spoken and written languages had to be made "more different" from each other than they were. This, India has attempted to accomplish primarily through the Sanscritization of Hindi in print or in print-proximate speech. The classicization of Hindi, a language that was separately established only in the mid-1940s, is considered by most Hindi language planners to be a necessary and even a sacred responsibility and one which is very much in accord with India's age-old values and traditions. If there are any questions remaining in this connection, they pertain to the degree of Sanscritization, rather than to whether Sanscritization is necessary or desirable at all.

Of course, the modernization of Hindi is greatly influenced by English too. However, this is a foreign and, ultimately, questionable influence (even though it is still co-official) and one that only Sanscrit can combat, hold at bay, and overcome. Were it not for Sanscrit, some believe, India would soon return to the cultural and linguistic "colonialist" subservience of the British raj, rather than become the cultural center of Asia and beyond, in accord with its self-perceived true destiny. The question is whether India is willing to undertake the great challenge of serious Sanscritization, rather than whether the challenge is really great and worthy of the spirit of India. This is also, more or less, the perceived nature of the challenge of classicization more generally, as the route to modernization in the other contexts in which a truly classical language lies at the classical heart of a nation's culture. This may be least so in the case of Hebrew, but even there the problem exists and burns in many hearts.

Hebrew/"Israeli"

Vernacular modern Hebrew is only about a century old and, therefore, it has not had much time to develop away from the classical model, which had preserved it for millennia in the functions of prayer, oral scriptural commandments, the study of classical religious texts (Old Testament and, particularly, Talmud) and rabbinic response and expository texts. The first two functions were intended for the Jewish "everyman" and, therefore, the Hebrew of these functions remained particularly fixed. The last three functions were heavily dependent on texts in Judeo-Aramic, which developed as a Jewish vernacular just before the early Christian era and continued to change thereafter, as do all vernaculars. For some 1,500 years or more, during which it too underwent devernacularization, it largely continued to involve only advanced students and rabbis. The two languages together (Biblical Hebrew and Judeo-Aramic) are considered as one within the Jewish tradition. Together they are *Loshn (ha)Koydesh* (the holy tongue or the tongue of holiness), but it is primarily the Biblical Hebrew component thereof that was widely known and in daily active use, at least by almost all males above the age of 13, and, therefore, became the major contributor to the protective "cocoon" that preserved the classical tongue for its "wake-up call" in the late 19th century, when political Zionism appeared on the scene, first in Central Europe and then in Eastern Europe, where Jews were overwhelmingly speaking Yiddish.

It is that "wake-up call" which is meant when the "revival of Hebrew" (which should really be called the "revernacularization" rather than the "revival" of Hebrew) is popularly referred to (see Fig. 6.3). And because we are now only a century or so beyond that point, the revernacularized variety (here called Israeli) is really a very young entity and one that has broken out of its confinement in the Biblical Hebrew fold and has borrowed substantially not only from other varieties within the Loshn Koydesh complex, but from other Semitic languages and, most recently, also from European languages (initially German, Russian, Pol-

FIG. 6.3.   Eliezer ben-Yehuda (1858–1922) The major early
Revernacularizer of the Hebrew language, favored a continuation of
classicist and Semitic emphases in his modernization efforts.
He even classicized his own last name from its original "Perelman"
and founded The Academy of the (Hebrew) Language (1890,
INITIALLY: "Language Committee").

ish, and, most particularly, Yiddish) and, ultimately and increasingly, from American English as well.

The Academy of the Hebrew Language, which is legally charged with updating this language for all functions of everyday modern life, initially carefully adhered to the line of "classicization", but its recommendations and preferences were so widely disregarded (if not ridiculed) for doing so that it has virtually eschewed its previous prescriptive *modus operandi*. It has concentrated more and more of its funds and efforts on the preparation of *The Great Dictionary of the Hebrew Languages*, intended to be an etymological and historical dictionary covering all ages and stages of the language and, therefore, not prescriptive at all. The age of language planning that was initially so vital for the vernacularization of Hebrew is now effectively over and the renaming of the language by some (as "Israeli") is intended to convey that realization (Zuckerman, 2003).

THE CLASSICIZATION CONTINUUM

Arabic, Sanscrit, and Hebrew are at three different stages along a continuum within the total language-planning process. Sanscrit is still called on repeatedly in the modernization of Hindi (and, to large extent, also in the modernization of all of the other major Sanscrit-derived vernaculars of Northern and Central India). These vernaculars, including Hindi, are well established and under authoritative language-planning supervision. There is no need to fear the demise of any but the smallest among them. Sanscrit is widely studied and some proportion of the populace even claims it as a mother tongue. However, although this claim is almost certainly an "error of admiration", it nevertheless reflects the fact that many of those who have acquired it through long and intensive study are now able to use it vernacularly and may, indeed, do so in small communities of their own. Nevertheless, no intergenerational transmission of vernacular Sanscrit has been reported on a societal basis and, accordingly, the true vernacularization of Sanscrit has not (yet) been attained.

Classical Arabic has also not been revernacularized. On the other hand, no local Arabic dialects are written, nor even spoken, for formal, cultured purposes. The most that has been attained along the route to vernacularization is the use of several regionally different varieties of Modern Middle Arabic, sometimes referred to as Standard Modern Arabic, although this designation may hide more than it reveals. "Middle" implies that these are compromises between the local educated vernaculars and Classical written Arabic. These have succeeded in finally making spoken regionwide communication possible and increasingly used on the radio, television, and in addresses by governmental authorities. These Middle Arabics (in the Maghreb, in and around Cairo, in and around Damascus, etc.) are also beginning to have preliminary but popular written functions, but this has not yet received any normative approval, probably for fear of ultimately forcing a split in the uniformly written Classical Arabic tradition that has lasted for over a millennium. As long as this continues to be the case, it must be said that written Arabic has not entered into the corpus planning process as fully or as seriously as have the major regional languages of India. The latter are utilized for formal spoken and written education at all levels, including the very highest, and they are (as they have long been) the vehicles of extensive folk, technical, and belletristic literatures.

In modern secular life, Hebrew has emancipated itself almost entirely from its classical origins and from the formal authorities that still pretty much controlled its modernization along approved channels as recently as half a century ago. In its current, more liberated guise, it has begun to be referred to as "Israeli". In the uninterrupted classical guise of traditional religion-dominated society, it is often still referred to as Loshn (ha-) Koydesh, or even as Ivris, giving a Yiddish-related twist to its secular designation (Ivrit), in recognition of the fact that in Ultra-Othodox circles, its phonology has been kept entirely identical to that of the community's continued vernacular use of Yiddish. Thus, only part of Israeli Jewish society is still within the penumbra of Classical Hebrew, increasing emergence from that penumbra becoming the norm for secular Israeli life as a whole. Where the latter circumstances obtain, there is a notable increase (and a constantly growing one) in the Americanisms that have infiltrated Israeli speech (and, to a lesser extent, writing).

Thus, classicization is not an all or none affair. Indeed, the other extreme of its bipolar opposite, "panification", the examination of which we now turn to, often maintains that it has a nodding acquaintance with classicization.

REGIONALIZATION VIA PAN-LANGUAGES

"Pan-" languages are intended to unite several polities that presumably have "common interests" (or "common problems") via the adoption of a single language or "super language" for the purposes of their more effective cooperation and, ultimately, political and cultural unification. However, instead of adopting or revising a current *lingua franca* or creating a brand new one, the unifying link in "panification" is purported to have existed in the remote past, now lost in the mists of prehistory, a link now waiting for reconstitution and a new call by the persons responsible for reconstitution to resume the greatness that was formerly their collective patrimony. Such a language planning venture shares with classicism the fascination for antiquity, but, if anything, the antiquity of the lost pan-languagee can be even older than in the "classical" case and its exact geohistorical borders are, therefore, ever so much more uncertain and "interpretable".

Some Pan-Languages That Were
(or "Could/Should" Have Been)

The contrasts between classicism and "panification" can often be more numerous and more edifying than has heretofore been widely assumed. *Classicization* involves the retention and renewed development of a very concrete variety of great immediate relevance to a particular people and polity whose sole or major vernacular it had been during that people's well-documented, although long-past greatness. *Panification*, on the other hand involves a threefold leap of faith: (a) the *reconstitution* of the hypothetical historical unity of now separate political entities; (b) the *recovery* of their hypothetical historical greatness during that former period of hypothetical unity; and (c) the functional *renewal* of the hypothetical common language of that hypothetical unity and greatness. Obviously, the triple decker of "hypotheticality" does not provide much hard and fast grounding for the many instances of panification that have dotted human sociocultural endeavors, but the recurring nature of such efforts gives testimony to the appeal that "a great past" has had, and still does have, for those whose present is often viewed as deficient in comparison to a far past, one that may be somewhat mythical but none the less illustrious beyond contention.

Some Examples From European History

The famous "Strassburg Oaths" of 842 A.D., at which Charlemagne's empire was divided up between his three heirs, one receiving the Romance lands west of the Rhine, another the Teutonic lands east of the Rhine, and the third, the more bilingual lands along the Rhine, are witness that the development of European vernaculars for some of the functions of state and of church, and the decline of Latin in favor of languages that could be spoken by laity with full confidence and unquestioned identity, were already advanced by that time. Within one and the same family of orientation, both languages could still be well enough known for each prince to swear to the oath in the language of the other's polity, although in the former empire as a whole, this quickly became less and less the case, even among princes and clergy. The glory and greatness of Latin increasingly became a local inheritance (e.g., both Spain and France long considered themselves to be the particular heirs of the glories of Latin), and its revived use as a unifying language of all of Europe that lay within the boundaries of allegiance to the Western Church remained an attractive operative possibility for many churchmen in particular. The Germanic lands had much less claim to any unifying language, given that their languages were not even distantly derived from Latin and that they carried the onus of having brought about the destruction of the former Roman Empire. Thus it is not until much later, indeed, during the age of early modern nationalism, that pan-languages for different parts of Central and Eastern Europe were given serious consideration.

Genuine and Spurious Panification

The so called Holy Roman Empire (c. 800 to 1800 A.D.) and its successor, the dual monarchy of Austria and Hungary (1867–1918), long made some pretenses at a pan-German federation that would spread from the French border all the way to the Russian border. However, even as late as the mid-19th century, Germany was no more than a patchwork of fiefdoms, independent duchies, and principalities that constantly bickered among themselves and were no match militarily for the more powerful and politically unified neighbors that surrounded them.

Nevertheless, weakness is fertile ground for a pan-movement that promises future grandeurs via a return to ancient ones. Pan-Germanists focused not only on the "German heartland", but also lavished attention on the *Auslandsdeutsche* (Germans living in settlements outside of the Reich), whom the vicissitudes of history had abandoned in areas that once seemed destined to become parts of the greater Germany: Austria, Chechia, Slovakia, Western Poland, Alsace, and Switzerland (not to mention even more distant settlements along the Volga, in the South Slavic lands, Transylvania and the United States). Wherever German settlements had been torn away (or had wandered away) from the fatherland, they should be reunited with the heartland so that the German spirit (first and foremost recognizable via language and linguistic creativity in folk songs, folk tales, folk sayings, proverbs, riddles, etc.) should and could reign supreme, as it had once done wherever their tongue held sway.

The stunning German victory (under Bismark) over France in the Franco-Prussian War (1870–1871), almost immediately led to the reestablishment of a united Germany, for the first time since the Middle Ages. Thereafter, the early German successes on both the eastern front and the western front during World War I all seemed to foretell the realization of a long-postponed dream of pan-German reunification. This dream was easily co-opted by the Nazi movement of the late 1920s and the early 1930s. Although it initially succeeded in returning many "lost children (provinces)" to the German "fatherland", the defeat of Nazism by the mid-1940s clearly spelled the end of the latter enterprise too. Except for the reunion of post-World War II West and East Germany, pan-German sentiment on a larger geographic scale has hardly surfaced since then.

The question still remains, however, whether this entire German phenomenon represents a valid instance of a pan-movement within the language-planning orbit. Although some of its early 19th-century rhetoric is certainly evocative of the theme of focusing on reunification of dispersed and mutually estranged branches of a single people in order to create a reborn "Germaness" or "Germandom", it stops short of attempts to include other Teutonic peoples (even though the Nazis thought highly of other "Arian" peoples like the Scandinavians, they were still not as purely Teutonic as the Germans themselves). Nor does it now aim at the recovery and creation of a linguistic medium that could unify and facilitate a return to greatness for all members of the "master race". Indeed, the German/Nazi experience is little more than a racially charged extrapunitive and self-aggrandizing movement and deserves to be looked on as a horrible miscarriage of ethnonationalism rather than even as a false heralding of linguistic panification at all. Other pseudo-panification movements in Europe were Pan-Slavism (which was primarily a tool of Czarist Russian expansionism among the western and southern Slavs) and, in the nearby Near East and North-Eastern Mediterranean region, pan-Arabism (which collectively opposed Western colonialism but otherwise lacked any overriding political or linguistic unificatory stress). They can each (pan-Germanism, pan-Slavism, and even pan-Arabism) be found lacking on one or another dimension of the more genuine three-pronged movements of the linguistic panification kind.

CREATING THE ILLYRIAN LANGUAGE

Soon after the Napoleonic Wars came to an end, after the first quarter of the 19th century, the south-Slavic linguist, historian, and nationalist politician, Ljudivit Gaj (pronounced "guy") was searching for an identity around which Slovenians, Serbs, Croatians, Bosnians, and perhaps even Macedonians could unite and build an all-inclusive, mutually acceptable south- Slavic nation and culture. He hit upon the name, "Illyrian". Surprisingly enough, the name was sufficiently vague, inoffensive, and yet suggestive that it encountered sufficient acceptance (both as a language name and as an ethnocultural designation) to meet with encouraging initial interest from all concerned. The fact that no one, not even Ljudivit Gaj, the initial main mover and shaker of the Illyrian movement, could pinpoint either the place or the culture associated with Illyria-of-old with any precision caused no great embarrassment. Everyone who mattered had heard of the name, vaguely, and recognized that it somehow pertained ("roughly") to a part of the multilingual and multiethnic Balkans (see Fig. 6.4).

Indeed, the designation Illyrium for a portion of the north Adriatic coast goes back to pre-Roman days, but, except for a short-lived, independent Illyrian Kingdom in the third century B.C., its most usually recognized limits were those set by the Romans, who conquered it in

FIG. 6.4. Illyria, in a rare 17th century map, with its exact limits unspecified (as usual).

the second century, as one of their very first colonies outside of Italy. It later grew to include most of the Adriatic coast, most of its islands and many northern and eastern inland areas as well. The name then went into a long (c. 1500 year) hibernation until Napoleon explicitly revived the name as a region of his empire in 1809, in the fond hope that this name would excite local passions favorable to his quest to conquer Europe. However, with Napoleon's defeat, it was subsequently annexed by Austria in 1816, as the Illyrian Kingdom, the definitive establishment of its exact borders being postponed for quieter times and the settlement of more urgent matters of crucial interest to the great powers (see Fig. 6.5).

This period of quiet was exactly what Gaj was waiting for. He negotiated avidly with other leaders of the southern Slavs (all of them then subject to Austrian, Hungarian, Russian, or Ottoman rule). In these discussions, it became clear that Gaj was indeed captivated by the ideal of reviving the ancient Illyrian nation and language, out of which he believed that a distinctively southern pan-Slavic entity would rise again, bringing new glory and prominence to the fortunate heirs of its illustrious Illyrian designation (Despalatović, 1975). Anti-Russian politics on the part of Germany and alternatively either France or Britain also played into Gaj's hands and brought him additional support. The Herderian thinking of the time adored "the idea of Illyrian" because, although its norm was still so flexible that something truly unique could be made of it, nevertheless, it had not capitulated to any of its larger or smaller neighbors. Gaj used this quiet interim time to try to persuade first Serbian and then Croatian leaders to accept the Illyrian written standard that he was codifying (on the assumption that the unified spoken counterpart would somehow spring fully formed from it) because it was closer to their own slightly differing written standards. Gaj was understood to be "developing the grammatical skeleton of modern written Illyrian from the literary treasures of the distant and illustrious Illyrian past". There was widespread conviction at that time that the Illyrian mother tongue had already existed and that all that was now needed was to select one of many equally available spoken paths for its written systematization (Kohn, 1955) so that it could proudly enter the ranks of Slavic literary languages, as predicted by none less than G. H. Herder per se (see Fig. 6.6). This line of analysis of records of scraps of long-neglected spoken languages, discovery of their shared grammati-

FIG. 6.5. Memorial for Ljudivit Gaj, 1809–1871, father of a stillborn Illyrian Pan-Language to unite the south Slavs.

FIG. 6.6. Johann Gottfried Herder (1744–1803), "Protector" of the Slavs and "Father" of romantic nationalism.

cal patterns on the basis of such analyses, and formulation of a newly written standard out of such discoveries had already worked for several other late-modernizing languages in the Slavic and Afro-Asian folds and it could have worked for Illyrian too, but, alas, it was not to be. The "underlying" mother tongue could not be quickly ascertained and the emergent grammatical pattern didn't emerge. Worst of all, neither the Serbs nor the Croatians were seriously willing to unify around a not-yet-existent Illyrian standard, given the far more advanced state of their own evolving standardized written varieties. They played along with Gaj but refused to be the first to accept his "gift" of an Illyrian standard as their own. By the latter part of the 19th century, the story of Illyrian, a "could have been" language, again receded from language planning awareness, even in its own part of the world, and is almost completely forgotten there as well as elsewhere today.

A Few More Panification "Might Have Beens"

The fact that Illyrian failed to come into being as a South Slavic pan-language (and the additional fact that there are a few other such failed panification examples, namely Ahmed Sukarno's planned "Maphilindo" (Minogue, 1967, pp. 13–14; Kennedy, J., 1908, pp. 82–83), to unite (i.e., to reunite) Malasia, the Philippines, and Indonesia into the great Austronesian kingdom that supposedly had once constituted Majapahit in days of yore, and the "Dravidistan" movement, among others, that aimed to reunite all of southern (non-Aryan or Indo-European) South India via a Tamil-based pan-language (McCully, 1940; see Fig. 6.7), does not invalidate this type of effort from being included in our language-planning typological thinking today. The history of ideas is not merely the history of successful ideas. Indeed, unless the failures are better understood, the successes also cannot be fully understood nor differentiated from the failures.

There are probably a far larger number of successful pan-movements than meets the eye. Every successful case of "norm" redefinition and official implementation support for redefinition can rightly be viewed as a case of successful panification. There is no natural barrier nor anything more than rather minute differences between the Flemish on the Belgian side and the Dutch on the Netherlands side of the Belgium/Netherlands

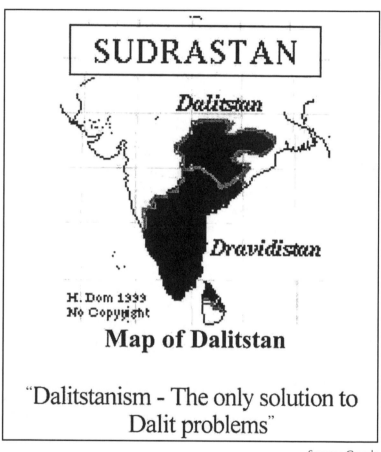

Source: Google

FIG. 6.7. Dalitstan, claimed as "The only solution to Dalit problems," nevertheless itself anticipated another, larger, Pan-Dravidian solution, unification with Dravidistan and the establishment of Sudrastan.

border. Nevertheless, there was for many generations a Flemish movement on behalf of the political independence and the linguistic officialization of Flemish speech from the varieties of the Waloon (and German) parts of Belgium. During this period, very few of the Flemish in Belgium or the Flemish in the western part of the Netherlands were impressed by the notion that the Flemishes of both countries were merely dialectal variants of the same Dutch language that united most of the Netherlands. Any ethnopolitical differences between the allegiances of their respective speakers were no more pronounced than those between speakers of other dialects of Dutch in the Netherlands as a whole. However, as a result of the Treaty of Vienna (1815) that brought the Napoleonic hostilities to a conclusion, the Netherlands Flemish and the Belgian Flemish found themselves on two different sides of a newly established and internationally recognized border. Indeed, the Belgian Flemish, Dutch Flemish, Belgian Germans, and Letzembergish speakers of Luxembourg could very well have constituted the bulk of a new pan-low-German confederation with an arguable claim to a long established written variety all its own. Perhaps such a variety would even have been extended to include Alsatian and Swiss German too in some future greater Lothringian union. This scenario did not come to pass, however, but the entire Dutch-low-German border of today is equally irrational and was/is not at all preordained by "the facts on the ground".

When dialectal unification is attempted or occurs within a small number of intrapolity jurisdictions (0-1), we tend to view that as merely part and parcel of the standardization process. However, when dialectal unification occurs across many political borders (on the assumption that the resulting larger and more inclusive borders correspond to those that existed formerly in some legendary golden past), then the necessary psychological and ethnocultural groundwork for panification become recognizable (see Fig. 6.8). The unification that we deem to be "simply" standardization is not at all that easy to arrive at; nor is the unification that we recognize as panification all that hard and improbable. Both require compromise and the definition of an acceptable model of the "good language" and, in both cases, that model will invariably be sociopolitically colored. Some linguistic varieties (like those within the Quechua, Aymara, and Mayan folds) can "go either way". Their current political boundaries do not mean very much to the speakers of any one of

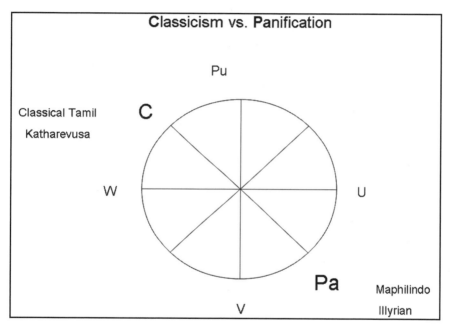

FIG. 6.8. Classicism vs. Panification.

these three varietal clusters but their amalgamation, either separately or jointly, is still rarely spoken of and a return to any presumed golden past is not likely to occur in the foreseeable future.

SUMMARY

The opposite poles of the classicization–panification dimension are in stark contrast to one another (as the diametrically opposite polls of a bipolar dimension should be). *Classicization* pertains to corpus planning that may be desired for the vernacular of an already united and recognized entity. Its classical poll pertains to the culture of a population that already recognizes its distinctive past communality, the classical, religion-imbedded, and religion-regulated maintenance of which is unquestioned (even by secular modernizers). Classicization varies in the degree to which (and in the speed with which) the currently spoken vernacular needs to be enriched by or displaced by the classical variety. *Panification* varies even more, however, and seeks to persuade diverse vernacular speakers of the relevance to their lives of a hypothetical classical with which it seeks to reconstruct and reconnect them. Obviously, the latter goal is a much more difficult task than the former and this may well explain why panification has had such a dismally low success rate. Even pan-Arabism, the classicization that stands closest to panification (perhaps because the related religious/written classical in this case was not in danger of being tampered with in any way) may have succeeded to the extent that it has no unified spoken/written substitute while it was being aimed at exclusively secular purposes and functions. Even so, panification has not yet been fully successful anywhere, in its task of unifying a far-flung constituency for attaining the requisite vernacular writing functions of modern daily life.

REFERENCES AND SOME FURTHER READINGS

Celan, P. (2004). *Todesfuge und andere Gedichte*. Suhrkamp, Frankurt A. M.
Despalatović, E. M. (1975). *Ljudevit Guy and the Illyrian Movement*. Boulder: Eastern European Quarterly.
Fishman, J. A., Conrad, A., & Lopez, R. (Eds.) (1996). *Post-imperial English*. Berlin: Mouton.

Fishman, J. A. (1963). Nationality-nationalism and nation-nationism. In J. A. Fishman, C. A. Ferguson, & J. Das Gupta (Eds.), *Language problems of developing nations* (pp. 39–52). New York: Wiley.

Kennedy, J. (1968). *Asian nationalism in the twentieth century*. New York: Macmillan.

Kohn, H. (1944). *The idea of nationalism: A study in its origins and background*. New York: Macmillan.

McCully, B. T. (1940). *English education and the origins of Indian nationalism*. New York: Columbia.

Minogue, K. R. (1967). *Nationalism*. New York: Basic Books.

Zuckerman, G. (2003). *Language contact and lexical enrichment in Israeli Hebrew*. New York: Palgrave Macmillan.

7

The *Ausbau* Versus *Einbau* Bipolar Dimension (or, Must the Lamb Look Unlike the Wolf in Order Not to Be Mistaken as Belonging to the Wolf?)

It is never good pedagogic policy to assign foreign designations to concepts being taught in English to primarily monolingual English-speaking students. Doing so runs the risk of making even the most relevant and lively topic seem distant and difficult. However, as already noted in connection with the "purity versus vernacularity" bipolar dimension, English has no strong corpus-planning bias against foreignisms and it doesn't take long for them to lose their foreign-markedness in English contexts, to feel perfectly "at home" there and to be regarded as perfectly good American (English) words, just as have "glitch", "sarong", "kamikaze", "kosher", "tomato", and so forth. And so it will also be, most Americans believe, with other "foreignisms": familiarity breeds respect, or, at least, the recognition that "no offense" has been either intended or taken.

THE "EVIL TWIN"

One disadvantage that contextually weaker language communities frequently seek to overcome via corpus planning is their actual (or even
just their perspectival) lowered status in the eyes of outsiders as writers
of "a mere dialect", in comparison to writers of their almost "identical"
stronger, better known, but evil twin. Dialect status, it will be remem-
bered, is a "put down", and it is felt as such mostly by the variety that is
most uneasy about its sociopolitical disadvantages. Thus, the fundamental problem is not whether B is "really a dialect of A" (or even why
A doesn't consider itself to be a dialect of B, because "similarity" obviously works both ways). Indeed, the Ausbau/Einbau relationship is not
one with which descriptive or typological linguists are really concerned. Linguists might actually prefer to classify the two varieties as
one, but their respective speech communities, Aian and Bian, are too
hostile toward each other and have been such for too long a time for
their accumulated grievances—particularly those of the more ag-
grieved party—to be lightly put aside, based on the evidence of "objec-
tive third parties". Actually, the stronger of the two might be quite
happy to swallow up the weaker as, indeed, the weaker party has often
suspected to be the case, but the latter adamantly insists on its independence, on the total legitimacy of its differences, and on the completely moral implications of its "departures" from its evil twin no
matter how tiny they may be, for even the most formal written functions. This fond goal of the weaker part is more easily hoped for than
attained and usually requires political separation in order to be implemented. This is precisely so because the basic issues are sociopolitical
and folk linguistic rather than purely linguistic per se.

How Does One "Build Away" One Language or "Variety"
From Another to Which it is Considered to Be Overly Similar?

The fundamental meaning of *Ausbau* is "building away" or distancing
one variety from another, The term expresses the sentiments of the ag-
grieved, weaker and less prestigious party, the one less widely encountered and recognized in print, the one most frequently "besmirched" as
being a mere dialect, to undertake steps that will increasingly differenti-

ate it from its rival. What kinds of differentiation and distancing are involved? In principle, linguistic distancing could be lexical, grammatical, orthographic, writing system related, numerical system involved, pronoun system involved, or pertaining to several of the aforementioned dimensions simultaneously. Let us review these possible dimensions of distancing via some actual cases.

We have already noted that the corpus planning activities of "language authorities" often seek to make the written and formal "exceptionality" characteristics (uniqueness) of their own language as unlike those of any other as they possibly can. We have also reviewed cases in which language authorities seek to distance their own language from a particular other language that enjoys worldwide ascendancy. We now turn to widespread cases in which the weaker of two neighboring languages that are very similar to one another undertakes to rid itself of the mistaken view that is no more than a dialect of its stronger neighbor, by making itself as different from that neighbor as it can ever be (Kloss 1967, 1993). This is a kind of "autonomy motivated distancing" that believes that all of its problems of a week language are derived from a "big brother" to which it is structurally, lexically, and in writing system very similar, indeed, so similar that its own independent status is thereby threatened. The efforts to overcome and decrease such similarity are called *Ausbau* ("building away" in German), while the efforts to foster and increase the similarity between the two (usually engaged in by the stronger party) are called *Einbau* ("building toward" in German). We start with the more common of the two, *Ausbau*, and then close this chapter with some examples of *Einbau* (see Fig. 7.1).

Croatian

Table 7.1 shows an alphabetic listing and a qualitative characterization of several cases of duos that stand in an Ausbau or in an Einbau relationship with one another. Starting off with Croatian (vs. Serbian), we note that three dimensions of distancing are involved. The pro-Croatian camp has relied on (a) finding, creating, and implementing lexical differences (often derived from the historically earlier rural dialectal origins of both languages), doing so especially for more learned and technical terms that Croatian may hitherto have lacked; (b) preferring

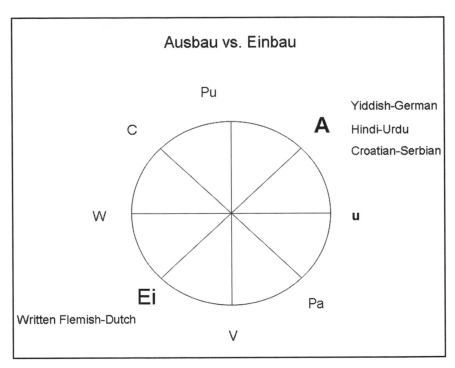

FIG. 7.1. *Ausbau* versus *Einbau*.

TABLE 7.1

Some Dimensions of Independence-Motivated Distancing (Ausbau) for 11 Cases of "Overly Similar" Duos

CASE	Lex	Gram	Spel	Writ	Num	Pron	& Einbau too?
Croatian vs. Serbian	X	X		X			Einb. concur
Flemish vs. Dutch	X	X	?				Einb. later
Indonesian vs. Maylay	X			?		X	Einb. later
Landsmal vs. Dano-Norwegian	X	X	X	X	X	X	Einb. later
Macedonian vs. Bulgarian	X	X		X			Einb. concur
Moldavian vs. Roumanian	X			X			Einb. later
Rusyn vs. Ukranian	X	X					Einb. reject
Slovak vs. Czech	X	X					Einb. prev.
Urdu vs. Hindi	X			X			Einb. reject
Valencian vs. Catalan[1]	X?		X?				Einb. reject
Yiddish vs. German	X	X	X	X			Einb. prev. + Einb. reject. later
Tot./dimen.	m11	7	m4	m7	1	2	

[1]In February 2005, the Valencian Academy of the Language voted to declare Valencian and Catalan to be two equally acceptable dialects of the same Catalan language. Whether nonlinguists in Valencia will be equally accommodating remains to be seen, particularly where governmental circles and the written language is concerned.

Note.   X = generally recognized and well documented dimension of Ausbau effort; ? = dimension is still unclear, unsure, or undocumented; m = maximally, i.e., counting the ?s.

Lex = lexical; Gram = grammar; Spel = spelling; Writ = writing system; Num = number system; Pron = pronoun system; Einb = einbau concurrently with rest of LP; prev = prior to rest of LP; reject = rejected.

grammatical constructions of longstanding rural currency but utilizing them in the written standard much more frequently than they had been hitherto utilized in the rural dialect; and (c) retaining the Latin alphabet that is so intimately connected with Croatian history, both ancient and modern. The quest for a single written (and "formal spoken") standard for both Croatian and Serbian was already a century old by the time World War I ended and an independent union of the South Slavs ("Yugoslavia") came into being. In this union, the Serbs (who had already gained their political independence from Turkey before the war) were demographically, economically, and politically ascendant, effectively controlling the new nation's language policies, purportedly compensating for their liberalism in connection with Slovenian, Macedonian, and Rusyn by being particularly vindictive vis-à-vis Croatian (see Fig. 7.2).

By the time Yugoslavia splintered and fell apart into its major ethnoculturally component parts, most of which, like Croatia, had never before attained the independent polity status that Serbia had already attained in the 19th century, the Ausbau aspirations of the Croatians had been effectively stymied.

They had been forced to accept (a) the designation "Serbocroatian", that is to give up their own independent name for their language and, therefore, its independent existence; (b) to forego many of the lexical and grammatical differences which could help differentiate their own formal written style from that of Serbian; and (c) accept a bogus "freedom of alphabets" constitutional provision in Yugoslav language policy (this in a country that had no freedom of speech!), whereby both Croatian and Serbian (or any other of the country's languages) could be written/printed in either the Latin or Cyrillic writing system. In this fashion, even a visual recognition of Croatian independence was denied (Greenberg, 2004). No wonder then that the newly independent Croatia lost no time to repeal all of the indications of Einbau and to insist that its "national language" was a free and independent entity that could and would make all decisions as to its present and future functions and structures entirely by itself. Furthermore, similar Ausbau decision on the part of Bosnia, Montenegro, and, perhaps even Herzegovina may ultimately result in there being five nominally independent ethnolinguistic entities, where there were previously only two or even just one (Ford, 2002). In that case, how different will or must these entities be in order to be

Source: Google

FIG. 7.2. Yugoslavia, before it splintered into its major ethno-regional components, as the 20th century drew to a close.

recognized as different? That, however, is a political issue and depends not on the degree of linguistic difference between them, but, rather, on the political power and on the degree of motivational consensus of their respective opposing claimants.

Yiddish (vs. German)

No one doubts that Yiddish is a Germanic language, as are English, Dutch, and Danish. Also, as in the case of English, Yiddish is a fusion language and, as such, it fuses together many "ingredients" from various other language families, for example, in the case of Yiddish, from Hebrew, various Slavic languages, and English, in particular. However, besides the Germanic ingredients that were part and parcel of Yiddish *ab initio*, from the very outset, roughly 1,000 years ago, when Jews first began to speak it to one another within Jewish cultural milieus and for the concepts and cultural pursuits of those milieus, "New (High) Germansms" were also admitted into Yiddish in more recent centuries. Over the course of time, the speakers of Yiddish immigrated, freely, by invitation, or through compulsion, eastward into the Slavic lands where they were also exposed to non-Germanic linguistic influences as well. However, even there, new German words again entered Yiddish (particularly in the 19th century) and these New High Germanisms became bones of contention when Yiddish underwent its own modernization, after spending centuries in mostly Slavic Eastern Europe.

The modernizers of Jewish life split into two camps in Eastern Europe. One camp (let us call them "the Germanizers") strongly favored the further importation of New High Germanism into Yiddish for the purposes of more rapid and more thoroughgoing Jewish Westernization. Several factors worked in their favor: German was not only widely admired by Eastern European Jews and non-Jews alike, as a uniquely appropriate language for the purposes of modernization (Westernization, Europeanization), not only because of its well- deserved reputation for highly developed science and technology, but it was close at hand (indeed, Germany itself lay only just across the border) and Jews had a head start advantage in learning it because their own vernacular, Yiddish, was quite similar to German in many respects. Thus, many Jewish intellectual leaders (rabbis, writers, journalists, teachers) favored the *Einbau* (i.e., the "building toward") of Yiddish into German, even before any serious Ausbau efforts were devoted to it (Schaechter, 1977).

The "anti-Germanizers", however, like *Ausbau* advocates everywhere, believed that it was possible for their kinsman to become modernized and yet reach this goal in their own vernacular and by a route that combined what was best in their own classic tradition with selected new knowledge, attitudes, and skills of the modern West. Hadn't all of the already Westernized nations themselves (England, France, and even Germany itself) walked along such an indigenously genuine and self-respecting path without losing their own individuality in the process? Weren't all of their immediate neighbors (Poles, Ukrainians, Byelorussians, not to mention "Slavophile" Russians) also attempting this more difficult but more "true to thine own self" solution of navigating between the foreign West and their own more slowly changing indigenous tradition?

How did the various anti-Germanizers (advocates of Ausbau) foster the ultimately greater success of their own convictions? They had no state apparatus of their own to rely upon; however, they did have intellectuals and protonationalist intellectuals aplenty, individuals who had spent years in the West and had returned from it unbroken, unspoiled, and "unsullied", with more dedication than ever to serve their own people via their own Yiddish vernacular (Fishman, 2004) (see Fig. 7.3).

Under the slogan *"avek fun daytsh!"* ("keep away from German") they published dictionaries (often bilingual ones at that) that steered the users away from unnecessary New High Germanisms by offering terms of newer or traditional vintage that standard German did not possess. They agreed on a unified revised spelling that was not beholden to German orthographic principles, but they turned down recommendations of adopting a Western, rather than a "Jewish", writing system as carrying things too far. They published lists of "words to avoid"; they published intellectual and scientific books, journals, and newspapers written in the modern "authentic" (i.e., anti-Germanist) style. They opened communally supported schools, largely elementary but, in some cases, also secondary and even tertiary schools, that consistently aimed at fostering an *Ausbau*-oriented, formal written style (D. Fishman, 2005). Since, with the rise of Nazism, the image

"More German" *im* vs. "Less German" *em* (before WWII).

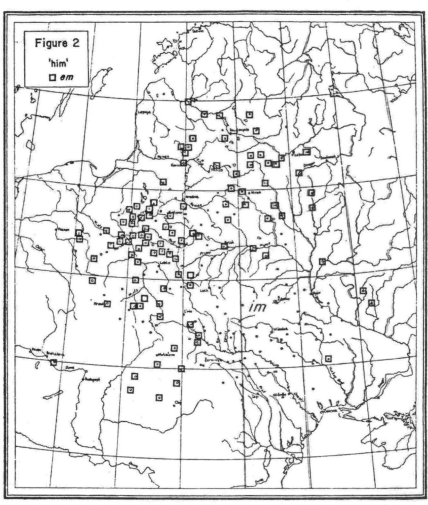

Source: M. Schaechter. 1969. "The Hidden Dimension in Yiddish language planning," M. Herzog, ed. *The Field of Yiddish*, v. 3. The Hague, Mouton, p. 289.

FIG. 7.3. Even though most Yiddish linguists espouse Ausbau, the more-Germanlike form is still frequently the more widely utilized one.

of all things German shifted radically for Jews, the *Ausbau* efforts on behalf of Yiddish have been carried further to this very day, albeit by a much reduced company of stalwarts (Fishman, 2004). Ausbau has "triumphed", so to speak, in the modern-secular Yiddish sector (if, indeed, there can be any "triumph" in orthographic change or lexical and syntactic innovation after a holocaust), whereas the pro-Germanizers, strangely enough, survive in the ranks of the Ultra-Orthodox alone, who largely remain oblivious to the *Ausbau/Einbau* tale told here.

The Turn of the Wheel

It would take up too much space in this brief presentation, were we to discuss each of the other nine cases listed in Table 7.1 (any one of them would be a fine homework or term-paper assignment, and there are plenty of other cases, including some in Latin America and in Africa, so that each student can examine one and report on it), but even from the two cases already discussed, it should be obvious that *Ausbau* and *Einbau* are not simply opposites; they are very often sequentially linked and that reveals an important trait of human nature and, therefore, of socially-sensitive language planning. The frequently sequential linkage between *Ausbau* and *Einbau* efforts is a reflection of their political nature, because politics by its very nature is confrontational. Power often changes hands and sometimes one side and then another ("the other") side controls the language-planning process and its direction. The tension between Macedonian and Bulgarian goes on today (the Bulgarians claiming that Macedonian was, is and always should remain merely a dialect of Bulgarian). So does that between Urdu and Hindi (the continued modernization of the latter still being guided by Sanscritization while that of the former is guided by Perso-Arabization, so that both "twins" will not become ("perish the thought!") mutually comprehendible and even interchangeable in their written guises. Valencian and Catalan have recently reached (indeed, while this book was being written in early 2005) a new high-point in their altercation, marked by rallies, marches, conferences, and Web sites, to either consensually declare their basic independence or their equally "obvious" (obvious to Catalanists) dialectal relationship to one another (see Fig. 7.4). Given the strong differences of opinion in each of these cases (the differences

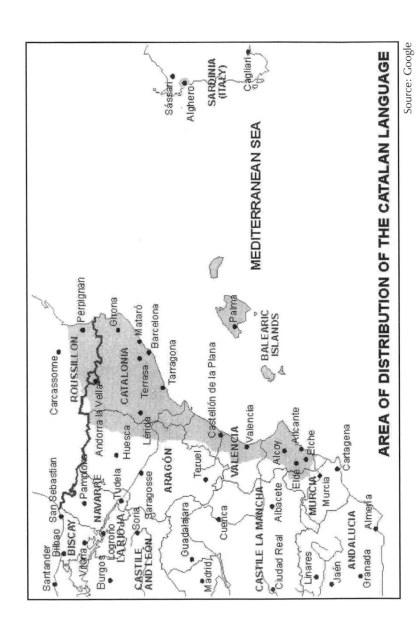

FIG. 7.4. Is there (or should there be) a language border, a dialect or no line at all seperating Catalan and Valencian?

often involving the [potential] political destinies of the polities involved), reversals of tactics or of strategies are always possible given the waxing and waning of the power differentials between the parties. Of course, in some cases, both processes go on simultaneously, *Ausbau* supporters and *Einbau* supporters are both determined to leave no stone unturned to gain or control any possibly advantageous turn of events. For the time being, the Catalanists have won, but the Valencianists have not entirely surrendered.

Ausbau/Einbau preferences and convictions are not merely examples of stubbornness or inability to compromise, but they are examples of some of the longest durational problems in the corpus-planning realm. That is because there is much more than only corpus planning at stake. Corpus planning inevitably coexists with status planning and the latter involves the retention or surrender of relative social power as well as the stability of one's most treasured ideals and commitments. Language loyalty, political loyalty and ideological loyalty all combine to make *Ausbau/Einbau* preferences among the most sensitive and closely interwoven areas of the total identity repertoire within many modernizing societies.

Q: Is Spanglish a case of Ausbau or Einbau? Read Stavans (2003): *Spanglish: The Making of a New American Language.*

The societies involved retool and refurbish their varieties so that they can appear to function proudly and on par with other "proper" Western languages. Once glimpsed, this is not a goal that any self-respecting variety is ever likely to surrender voluntarily, just in order to "get along". However, like all policies, it exacts a price and its price must be compared with its payoff, to determine which is the greater of the two. We may not be adept at measuring either of these two, the costs and the benefits, particularly if we include their crucial psychic and sociocultural dimensions. However, we are not free to ignore them entirely either, because they are most certainly there, whether or not we can measure them with sufficient sophistication or accuracy. Their consequences were and are very real relative to the lives of those individuals and societies on which they impinged.

Had there been no *Ausbau* there would have been no *Landsmål* (see Fig. 7.5); had there been no *Einbau*, there would have been no *Samnorsk*. Had there been no movement for *Ausbau* there would have been no Croatian after half a century under Serb domination, and no Macedonian vis-à-vis Bulgarian, and no Rusyn vis-à-vis Ukrainian. The thrilling trajectories of the mutual *Ausbau* of Hindi and Urdu (Fig. 7.6), and of Moldavian vis-à-vis Romanian would never have transpired and without *Ausbau* Yiddish would never have undergone secular modernization, just as without *Einbau* it would not still be struggling against New High Germanisms even today. Finally, not only are both *Ausbau* and *Einbau* very real, one might say even "momentous" enterprises for many languages throughout the world, but they give us a more realistic and more nuanced picture of the power of language planning as a whole, and of corpus planning in particular, to enable human societies and cultures to alter their languages and to actually make them more like what they really want them to be vis-à-vis particular neighbors. Languages need no longer feel locked into place for all eternity.

The realization that the future of the characteristics of their language is in their own hands can be either a powerfully liberating or aggrandizing experience for the peoples of the modern, globalizing world. The degree of sameness and the extent of differences between languages can now be influenced by human actions and preferences, rather than left up to the pleasure of the gods alone. Like every other power that humans have come to possess in modern times, *Ausbau* and *Einbau* can be used for purposes of good or evil, for equality and democracy or for inequality and totalitarian rule. The choice of how *Ausbau* and *Einbau* will be used is up to human societies, their values, and their language authorities. Knowing that should make us all more aware that an increased power over language is an increased responsibility for those who control or can influence this power to do so not only for their own good, but for the good of their neighbors, and for the good of humanity more generally. In this respect, corpus planning is no different from any other tool that enhances human control over the environment; every increase in human power requires a corresponding increase in human responsibility relative to the uses and users of that power.

FIG. 7.5. An anti-Landsmål (Nynorsk) cartoon, depicting it as an unbelievably old, backward and hideous monster from which civilized city-fold seek to escape.

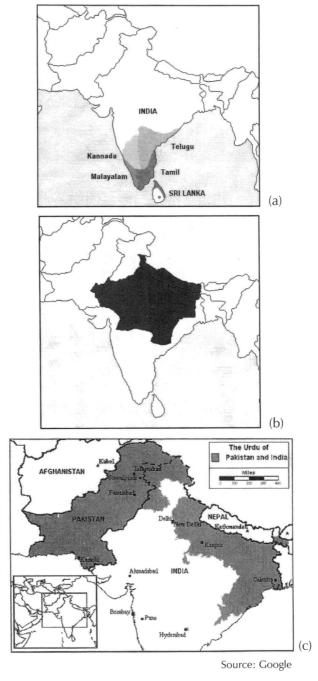

Source: Google

FIG. 7.6. The three major language families of India
(a) Dravidian languages, (b) Hindi languages ("Indo-European")
and (c) Urdu in India and Pakistan.

REFERENCES AND SOME FURTHER READINGS

Fishman, D. E. (2005). *The rise of modern Yiddish culture.* Pittsburgh, PA: University of Pittsburgh Press.

Fishman, J. A. (2004). Yiddish and German: An on-again, off-again relationship (and some of the more important factors determining the future of Yiddish). In A. Gardt & B. Huppauf (Eds.), *Globalization and the future of German* (pp. 213–227). Berlin: Mouton.

Fishman, J. A. (in press). Yiddish language planning and standardization. *The YIVO Encyclopedia of Jews in Eastern Europe.*

Ford, C. (2002). Language planning in Bosnia and Herzegovina: The 1998 Bihac Symposium. *Slavic and Eastern European Studies, 46*(2), 349–361.

Greenberg, R. D. (2004). *Language and identity in the Balkans: Serbo-Croat and its disintegration.* New York: Oxford University Press.

Kloss, H. (1993). Abstand languages and Ausbau languages. *Anthropological Linguistics. 35*(1-4), 158–170.

Schaechter, M. (1977, Fall). Four schools of thought in Yiddish language planning. *Michigan Germanic Studies, 3*(2), 34–66.

Stavans, I. (2003). *Spanglish: The making of a new American language.* New York: Rayo.

8

The Interdependence
and Independence
Dimensional Clusters

Having reviewed four bipolar dimensions and eight poles in the corpus planning of written language (and, therefore, eight "poles" in all), the reader may be happy to learn that no additional bipolar dimensions will now be introduced. There may, indeed, be more, because the differentiations that can be made in orthogonal multidimensional space are, at least theoretically, endless, but the differences between them conceptually are likely to become progressively smaller and smaller, on one hand, and parsimony too has much to be said for itself, on the other hand. Ever since the very earliest scientific arguments, two quite different goals have beckoned to the practitioners of science: parsimony (remember *Occam's razor*?), and exhaustiveness ("multidimensionality"). Corpus planning also has appealed to both of these goals and, in fact, has often done so simultaneously. Societies are very complex organisms, particularly free societies, who can take off in any and all directions at any moment, and no single approach will ever satisfy all of them.

THE INDEPENDENCE CLUSTER

The simplest (most parsimonious) possible partitioning of eight bipolar dimensions is into two superdimensions or "higher order factors". One of these factors that seems pertinent to corpus planning might consist of different degrees of input from the purity, uniqueness, classicism, and *Ausbau* dimensional poles. What is it that these four have in common? It seems to be the momentum (a preference or bias) toward separating or distancing "the beloved language" from others that impinge upon it. Purity, uniqueness, classicism ad *Ausbau* all share a common goal: to foster the "authentic individuality" of the spirit and the substance that has rendered one's own language exactly that: "one's own and no one else's". This can be a powerful motive, indeed, particularly for language communities that are or have long been considered "ugly ducklings". Every late modernization movement (and every language movement that is or has been "late" relative to certain others in its vicinity), every contextually weak language movement (and every language movement that is or has been "weak" relative to certain others in its environment), every corpus planning movement that co-exists with other collective efforts that are marked by elements of nationalism or ethnocentricism, have or have had a strong dose of "independence" stress in their corpus-planning dynamics.

As with individuals who want nothing more than they want "to be free to be themselves", societies under threat and political cultures under attack may, particularly during times of stress, want "to be free to be themselves" (or think that is what they want) more than anything else that is on their agenda. However, there is rarely a time when that is really all they want.

The Interdependence Cluster

Independence is well and good, but in some of life's myriad pursuits a strong dose of interdependence is also a definite asset. The successful pursuit of truth through science may well constitute one of the latter, because few, indeed if any, politicocultural establishments posses the requisite manpower and brainpower to successfully pursue all types of scientific advances in isolation. Scientific concepts, procedures, and advances are the true common property of humanity as a whole, as is the very vocabulary of scientific progress as a whole. Science ultimately tears down borders rather than erects them and the fraternity of its practitioners is both highly interactive across political boundaries and cooperative by experience. More so than in any humanistic field of endeavor, advanced scientific endeavors maximize replicability and shared notational languages. As such, corpus planning for science and technology tends toward worldwide formalization and standardization, that is, toward shared interdependence across political and cultural boundaries.

Corpus planning for science/technology functions seeks both common vernacularity at the spoken level, as well as proximity to or identity with the vernacular of the best established "scientific" nomenclatures. Similarly, it pursues shared uniqueness, classicism, and *Ausbau* at the written level. Accordingly, science worldwide has invested heavily in English journals, conferences, and symposia, no matter in which part of the globe they are pursued. Indeed, science presents us with an anomalous profile: a corpus planning profile of its own kind of interdependence: an "independent interdependence" (unlikely though that may seem) of considerable visibility and power. Other domains that can be similarly described as having a status-planning strategy all their own (and therefore not being tied to that of their polities in other pursuits) are upper-level technology, commerce, and big-business. In these particular pursuits, interdependence rules the roost, even when that is not necessarily the case for their polity's corpus planning policy as a whole. (See Fig. 8.1 and Fig. 8.2).

The combined implications of the "always-still-incomplete" nature of both the independence and the interdependence clusters is that corpus planning is like a "mixed economy": it may not only fluctuate from time A to time B, but it may also fluctuate from one functional domain to another within each time. There are many possible way-stations between "proud isolation" and "principled interdependence". In either case, a change in direction as well as a change in emphases may be tactically called for. However, surprising though it may seem, no official change may be necessary at all when corpus-planning reversals occur, but, rather, merely a change in the inclusiveness of the range of corpus planning desiderata as a whole.

THE WORLD IS VERY MUCH WITH US

Is it possible for languages to be entirely inward oriented? If so, what would be the realistic functional profile of such languages? Languages

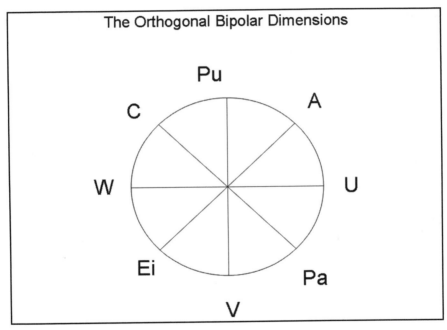

FIG. 8.1. The orthogonal bipolar dimensions.

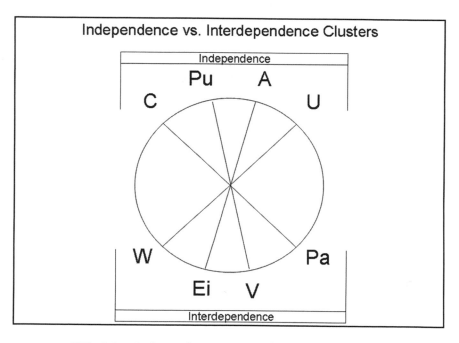

FIG. 8.2. Independence vs. interdependence clusters.

cannot be untouched by their functions, for their functions give them shape, purpose, and meaning. Human cultures are what they do, think, feel, and their languages are very much a reflection of the functional needs that they have been put to, have grappled with, and have expressed, but, also, of the particular values, styles, and preferences that cultures have developed for their grapplings. Cultures are both goal-oriented and means-oriented and their language(s) are constituted by both goals and means.

Languages foster sociocultural interaction within cultures and between cultures. As a result, they satisfy and express both acts of independence and of interdependence. The bipolarity of corpus planning is implemented (not necessarily equally, but nevertheless, without fail) in order to provide all languages with all possible opportunities for successful multidirectionality. They are complex tools for complex communities and, as a result, are ready both for navel gazing and for star gazing, even if one is engaged in daily by all, and the other is engaged in rarely by few. The directional inequality of cultures is a fact of existence, but it has, therefore, consequences for languages that corpus planning may be utilized to "correct", either direction being available for further elaboration at any time that any subgrouping of users so requires. As a result, languages are not functionally equivalent at any particular time, just as they are not culturally equivalent, but they are potentially all repairable wherever gaps in attained versus desired functionality are recognized and the repair of these gaps is authoritatively undertaken.

9

Can Opposites and Incommensurables be Combined?

"Having one's cake and wanting to eat it too" is such a common human trait that we could not be far off to assume that it is a common trait in connection with corpus planning also. Indeed, this is actually so. We have just noted that many polities (e.g., India) pursue the independence cluster when engaging in corpus planning for the humanities and social sciences, while opting more for the interdependence cluster in connection with the natural sciences.

Religion is a notable domain whose corpus planning is more often obviously discontinuous in comparison with others. Religion deals with eternal verities that were commonly stressed in ages long past, before modern econotechnical domains achieved anything like their current importance or even dominance in human affairs. Religions frequently possess unchanging, nonvernacular, and hallowed texts the preparation and standardization of which can go back to well before recorded history. In addition, the faithful "performance" of these texts is commonly considered more crucial than their understanding of or even than the grasping of their general gist. The hallowed is commonly viewed as essentially eternal and performance oriented, therefore without any necessity for public comprehension on a literal or even semiliteral basis.

Accordingly, the languages of religion in modern times are often discontinuous—more classical, "purer", differently written—than the language(s) of everyday life more generally.

There are sometimes other differences as well. The language(s) of religion are frequently mediated via other languages in order that they too may be rendered (more) comprehendible and, therefore, they (the mediating varieties) customarily influence their co-occurring vernacular or mirror images more strongly than do the older religious varieties per se. For all of these reasons, the varieties directly associated with the mediation of sanctity may be come to be looked upon as *co-sanctified vernaculars*, rather than as vernaculars pure and simple. They occupy a middle rank in venerability, as does the King James version of the English Protestant bible in the English speaking world, or the various guides to comprehension used by Moslems during services throughout the world (even though their language of audible prayer is most frequently Koranic Arabic), or the varieties of Sanscrit utilized by Hindus, the variety of Yiddish long used in translating the Bible (Old Testament only) in traditional (orthodox) Hebrew school or home instruction for women and children.

All in all, when any culture devotes the major part of the school day for years on end to formal, translation-mediated study, the translation per se becomes the point of departure for a new language variety based on the grammar of the original calque variety and on endless translation calques, each of which followed the other over the course of centuries (often without the full discontinuation of its predecessor calque, which is then retained for ceremonial [commemorative] purposes only, rather than to promote comprehendability) (see Fig. 9.1).

Once again, it becomes clear that functionally opposite (therefore "discontinuous") varieties can be combined, not merely in terms of repertoire development, but in terms of intravarietal corpus planning. Nevertheless, the result is a smoothly functional whole, that is, a variety or repertoire that corresponds to a perspectival functional unit in which no contradictions or conflicts are apparent to the "insider", no matter how much "outsiders" wonder how this can be. We all live with and according to our own culturally integrated realities and this is so in the realm of language as much as in any other realm.

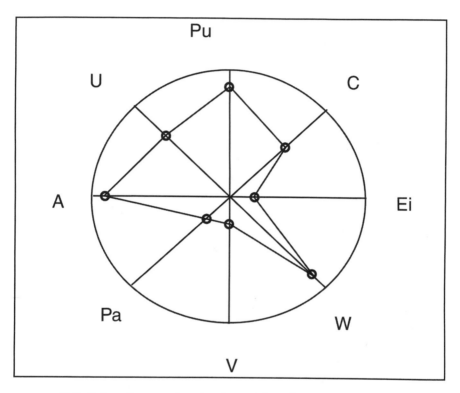

FIG. 9.1. Corpus planning for a calque language which has preserved its translation co-sanctity functions for a millennium or more and has simultaneously been undergoing serious modernization and *Ausbau* during the past century.

Opposites are always combinable when they are not avowedly interpreted as such. Sick prisoners on "death row" are first hospitalized and brought back to good health before they are executed. The political self-designation as "Christian socialists" is not viewed by others as an impossible contradiction in terms (notwithstanding the anticlericalism of most socialists). An expression that is half Germanic and half "Romanic", such as *Merci vielmals*, ("many thanks" in Swiss German) is not viewed as a hopeless jumble of discordant components—thankfully so; any more than in the case of English, which is overflowing with combinations of exactly this type (as are all fusion languages), "cordial thanks" for example.

Similarly, corpus planning proceeds to serve cross-functional purposes, such that Western sports and pop-culture interests, Eastern philosophies, and modern econotechnical pursuits are all available to the very same public (thereby calling upon vernacularization, classicization, and internationalization) without any implied or experienced incongruity. Ethnolinguistic establishments and their language "authorities" need not be internally conflicted or in complete "disarray" in order to adopt quite different corpus-planning directions (neither in polar opposite terms nor in dimensional terms) for the various functional pursuits of modern-day life.

Nevertheless, there need be no particular preset balance of directions in order to overtly announce a corpus planning policy (and to be viewed by the general public as providing such a policy) that favors one bipolar direction above others. The announced corpus-planning policy may be one of "purity" and yet international econotechnology may be exempted without comment or demurrer, from the policy strictures that are binding in other functional areas. Cultural pretenses in favor of established cultural verities are common in most cultures (escape clauses, "grandfathering" provisions in order to get a policy "moving", are all strategies well known to all of us). Corpus planning operates in accord with the general culture of legislation and implementation and, therefore, is also subject to all of its shenanigans as well. *Patterned evasion* (collectively claiming to do one thing while doing its opposite) did not have to wait until the field of corpus planning was invented in order to become part of the local linguistic and political culture.

All in all, corpus planning reflects all of the foibles of human nature, rather than runs counter to them, and we are a very contradictory species. Most particularly, however, corpus planning reflects the political culture that inevitably dominates it (just as do educational planning, industrial planning, business planning, school planning, demographic planning, and all other types of authoritatively sanctioned and conducted planning), as to exactly what are to be taken as real incommensurables and opposites (and when). Could corpus planning really do otherwise and would it be any more (or less) successful if it did? A greater or lesser decisional inconsistency may be its saving grace, its human grace.

10

Epilogue: Some Things OLD and Some Things NEW, and Some Things BORROWED on Which to Chew

We have been exploring a "new look" at corpus planning: one that strives to be more societally (than has hitherto been the case) than linguistically imbedded. Perhaps, as might have been expected, it has led not only to the development of a number of new formulations, but, also, to the confirmation of certain prior, well-established views and toward the disconfirmation of others. There seems to be nothing that is entirely "new under the sun".

The previously dominant view of corpus planning has considered this pursuit to be an entirely technical and professional endeavor, so much so, indeed, that the topic, as such, could hardly be presented in a time frame usually allotted to early postgraduate (let alone, undergraduate) courses. On the other hand, there was little time or space for anything that was conceptual about corpus planning, and, therefore, far too little time for very much that was conceptually or, indeed, that was cross-linguistically transferable or generalizable about it. Corpus planning was viewed as simultaneously highly language specific but it proceeded everywhere by merely following or depending on previously familiar models of "modernization and the good language" (Fishman 1983). However, the present analysis has pointed to various orthogonal and parsimonious sociolinguistic dimensions and clusters of dimensions that tend to make the corpus-planning topic both more understandable and more generalizable by relating its emphases to other major aspects and emphases of various everyday modern and modernizing cultures.

There is an important lesson to be learned from a sociolinguistic approach that starts off its inquiries with a consideration of the major convictions and deeply ingrained historical experiences that a large variety of speech communities throughout the world have brought to the corpus planning table. If there are alternative approaches that are possible in the pursuit of corpus planning, which should be given preference? Bluntly put, should the researcher begin with purely linguistic variables such as nasalization, pluralization, and vowel-harmony, for example, or with ideological and political variables that characterize the local modernization process per se, such as *Ausbau*, uniqueness, and vernacularization? Given that the investigator is invariably trying to account for as much variance as possible in the acceptance of corpus-planning proposals, our current discussion leads to the conclusion that broad-based, widely subscribed to societal dimensions should be considered first. They are much more likely to account for appreciably more variance in "acceptance" (and therefore, in liking, learning, and using corpus-planning "products") than will variables that are of a much narrower nature insofar as "man-in-the-street" implementation awarenesses are concerned. If thousands of man-in-the-street advocates are willing to (and sometimes even do) attend a week long symposium on the minutia of corpus planning for their own "beloved language", one can be sure that this is so not because they are really interested in the technical details of corpus planning but, rather, in the social change that corpus planning implies. The general maxim that applies here is "Do not use a scalpel to slice up a carcass until you are sure that the meat cleaver has been used to all possible advantage".

CORPUS PLANNING VERSUS STATUS PLANNING: IS THERE A VALID DIFFERENCE?

The aforementioned consideration also pertains to the fundamental distinction between corpus and status planning as a whole. If, for example, we have discovered that there is such a major status loading in corpus planning as a whole, then is the aforementioned distinction really a necessary one at all? How redundant are these two categories really, or is anything still left to be said for corpus planning per se. By way of reply, it is worth keeping in mind that overlap does not equal identity. A distinction is still worth retaining until it can be studied both separately and in interaction with other distinctions. Furthermore, any study undertaken to investigate the possibility of revealing hitherto hidden status dimensions within corpus planning does not provide the best perspective from which to consider the ubiquity (or its lack) of status planning per se, or the possibility that there may even be a hidden corpus dimension in status planning too. After all, when two dimensions overlap, *they overlap with each other*. An opening salvo does not win the battle and, indeed, is likely to leave many unsolved problems in its wake.

Because linguistically ordinary speakers (linguistically innocent folk-speakers) need to be enticed into and remain within the "corpus-planning positive" fold, it is clear why the folk-linguistic dimensions that we have proposed in this volume might become useful guides to the support, advocacy, and acceptance of such features by such speakers. Such features can more readily become (if they are not already) emic features (and, therefore the bases of collective implementational action) than are dimensions of a more strictly etic nature alone for the same speakers.

"Ireland: Not Only Free but Irish; Not Only Irish but Free!": The Best of All Possible Worlds

When the Irish revolutionary movement sought to attain the greatest possible mass following with respect to its radical political goals vis-à-vis Great Britain (in the late 19th and early 20th century), the Irish had already become primarily an English-speaking people for well over a century. Thus, the revolutionaries were faced with the dilemma of both

opposing English as their future national language and yet being constrained to use it constantly in order to communicate most effectively
with each other and with their own actual and potential followers. The
slogan that they developed, as cited in the heading to this section, clearly
implies the complexity and even the possibly internal contradictions
within any corpus-planning movement's program of action.

All of corpus planning (indeed, all of politics) must take a position
with respect to very similar set of dilemmas. Inconsistencies that are
self-discovered are still reparable, whereas ones that are first discovered
by the opposition may no longer be so easily coped with. The need to
reconcile opposites and yet to maintain any advantages that flow(ed)
from prior complete consistency is part and parcel of the internal dynamics of corpus planning. The seeming lability of corpus planning is
explained by the human condition; no single or completely adequate solution to the myriad problems that engulf us is ever available at one and
the same time. Thus, human societies inevitably vacillate between pro
and con, between the favored and the disfavored alternative, between independence and interdependence, and more democratic corpus-planning authorities vacillate not a whit less, but probably even more, than
do authoritarian ones.

The best of all possible "real worlds" includes both *Ausbau* and
Einbau. The struggle between them is most usually not one between full
rejection of autonomy-motivated distancing, on one hand, nor of full acceptance of it, on the other hand. The previously Francophone countries
of the Maghreb have combined the hard-won triumph of Arabic, since
the populist (and popular) expulsion of the French, with substantial use
of French (and/or even of English) in certain domains and for certain
preferred social and economic classes (e.g., in the schooling of the children of those very government functionaries in charge of corpus
Arabization). The erstwhile revernacularization of Hebrew is now faced
with Hebrew avoidance in popular signage and among many of the
young, stylish, and hip generation. This does not mean that corpus planning is, therefore, an entirely unprincipled sham. It does the best it can in
a cruel world in which few disadvantaged languages reach anywhere
near developmental maturity without learning the lesson that "He/she
who fights and runs away lives to fight another day!" Corpus planning
often repeats the same political tune again and again in one full cycle

after the other. But it does so out of a constant search for a fallback solution that may be effective for at least certain segments of its erstwhile supporters who are constantly estimating and recalculating their best chances, both for their children and for themselves.

"For the Good and Welfare"

The major point to have in mind about corpus planning is to try to see it not only from the ordinary speech-community member's perspective, but also to see it from the perspective of the societal "authorities" who are responsible for its formulation, motivation, and evaluation. These authorities almost certainly conceptualize their efforts as being a contribution to the improvement of the status quo for members of the group (industry, agency, district, governmental unit, or intergovernmental agency) on whose behalf they are engaged in corpus planning. If they are really public servants, then they should be evaluated primarily by the particular public whom they are ostensibly serving, and this should be done in accord with the usual norms of evaluation (of methods and outcomes) in effect in that particular "culture".

When viewed in such terms, it should become quite a bit clearer that the kind and direction of corpus planning, its rewards and punishments, its priorities and its pace, should all be seen in relative (i.e., in culture-bound) terms. Of course, cultures can and do evaluate one another, but until and unless there is a shared "culture of planning", such evaluations may be expected to show less consensus—just as do the cross-cultural evaluations of culture-specific art, music, philosophy, and morality—than do evaluations within a shared frame of reference.

Once we also see corpus planning from "the other's point of view" (or, at least, *also* from the other's point of view), we can appreciate that it is utilized in order to help strengthen collectivities of various sizes and resources and to assist them in overcoming some of their collective and individual problems and disadvantages. Strengthening the collective good and welfare may also, nevertheless, relatively disadvantage still other hitherto advantaged collectivities, for example, some of those who previously controlled most advantages and who must now share some of these with relative "Johnny-come-latelies". Since the world will probably always be marked by relative advantages and disadvantages on a variety of dimensions, then we must take care not to hold the weaker parties, including speech communities, "responsible" for any and all unanticipated consequences that flow (and that must flow) from their very human efforts to plan and to maximize the attainments of their very own constituencies. However, it is the weaker parties that ultimately must also take care not to engage in too much dislocative change, as most of the former Soviet states have learned the hard way in their initial drives to disestablish Russian.

However, it is because patrimonies are within (or very nearly so) the pale of sanctity (Durkheim, 2003), that the self-concepts and the collective identities of those who engage in and are charged with conducting corpus planning must be granted the benefit of the doubt. Basically, they deserve as much of the freedom and recognition of claiming that they labor in pursuit of maximizing "the general good and welfare" that we grant to ourselves, to our own authorities, and to our own cultural tone setters and goal setters.

The major conclusion that we seem to have arrived at is that corpus planning is full of intimations of status-planning goals and aspirations. There is no (and there can be no) sharp division between these two pursuits when they are both addressed from the point of view of intrasocietal definitions of what it is that corpus planning is really about functionally speaking, insofar as the wishes of its sponsoring community and their authorities. It raises the question, at every turn, of not only how corpus planning is conducted and by whom, but of the larger agenda, the sociocultural agenda to which language planning as a whole inevitably contributes and from which it derives the popular legitimization upon which its actions can be based.

CORPUS PLANNING AND IDEOLOGICAL NEUTRALITY

Is there no ideologically neutral corpus planning? Must it always be encumbered in one way or another? Cannot corpus planning merely pursue nonideological ("purely linguistic" or stylistic) goals, such as brevity, learnability, well-formedness, and word-paradigm fidelity? Of course it can, but there may be many several equally brief solutions to a given corpus-planning need and it is *in the choice among them* that linguistic culture plays its most distinctive goal. Were Esperanto, Ido, and other such IALs (international auxiliary languages) really neutral in their own corpus planning? If so, then why were they all so criticized for their purported "European" biases? A one-syllable "solution" to a corpus gap may exist from a "uniqueness" point of departure, from an "internationalization" preference, from an "*Ausbau*" point of view, from a "vernacularization" conviction, and so forth. It is in the choice among the above alternatives (as well as in the choice of doing no corpus planning at all) that cultural values and linguistic culture come into full play.

But, finally, aren't parameters such as the ones just mentioned nothing but "unscientific" folk-label considerations that language scientists should try to move speech communities away from, rather than utilize and dignify? However, where either popular linguistic culture is in full control or technical linguistic expertise is ascendant, there are potentially many ways in which the dictates of either can be satisfied. It is after the optimal linguistic culture solution has been selected, giving full voice to "bottom–up" popular participation approaches, that technical linguistic sophistication can best be called for, so as to be sure that corpus panning also fits into a consistent paradigm of the beloved language from a strictly linguistic point of view as well. Furthermore, it cannot be overly stressed that in order to understand language planning as a whole, one must also study status planning as well, or a volume that combines status planning and corpus planning together, in an integrated fashion.

If no corpus planning of any kind is pursued, that does not mean that no language planning is underway at all. First of all, "no policy" leaves whatever language is "in control" still in the "driver's seat" and, therefore, a "no policy" policy (e.g., with respect to designating an official language of the United States) is always a silent vote for the continuation of the status quo and of those who benefit thereby. Secondly, when no corpus-planning policy is underway that certainly does not mean the status-planning measures are not in place and rigorously followed.

In this introduction to corpus planning, we have stressed that corpus planning proceeds in accord with the more general politicolinguistic culture of the society that engages in it. How decisions are arrived at (top–down, bottom–up or both at various stages of the total language-planning process), how they are enforced, and, if necessary, repealed, modified, and evaluated, these are not, strictly speaking, corpus-planning considerations and, therefore, they have not been reıewed here. Nor have we devoted attention to the crucial question of differing degrees and kinds of language-planning "success", how they should be measured, among which segments of the population, and the relationship of "success" to the types of motivation and implementation available, on one hand, and the direction of corpus planning initially followed, on the other hand.

Our discussion in this text has been limited to corpus planning alone, not because it particularly deserves to be studied alone but because there is far less introductory literature available on this particular aspect of language planning than on status planning. It is the author's hope and intent soon to prepare an introductory text that will seek to address both of these major segments of language planning and to do so within a single integrated framework. A beginning along these lines has already been made (Fishman, 1980) and it now remains to revise, expand, and update that text for students and practitioners alike.

REFERENCES

Durkheim, E. (2003). *Sociologist of modernity.* In M. Emirbaye (Ed.), Malden: Blackwell.

Fishman, J. A. (1980). Bilingual education, language planning and English. *English Worldwide, 1,* 11–24.

Fishman, J. A. (1983). Modeling rationales in corpus planning: Modernity and tradition in images of the good corpus. In J. Cobarrubias & J. A. Fishman (Eds), *Progress in Language Planning* (pp. 107–118) . Berlin: Mouton.

Appendix 1

QUESTIONS FOR CLASS DISCUSSION OR WRITTEN ASSIGNMENT

1. Review Ilan Stevans' *Spanglish: A New American Language*, New York: Rayo, 2003. If you could do so, would you want to make Spanglish more like Spanish or more like English? How would you "organize" to get this accomplished?
2. Is fostering literacy via creating a writing system for a hitherto oral-only language an instance of corpus planning or of status planning?
3. Is there any kind of status change that does not require a corresponding corpus change.
4. What happens to corpus-planning innovations that have been introduced when expected or recently introduced status changes are canceled due to war or conquest or severe economic reverses? Can you think of any actual cases of this kind?
5. In what ways would American English benefit by (or be harmed by) an authoritative academy to foster its purity and uniformity (something like the *Service de la langue Francaise* does for Canadian French)? As the leader of the English speaking world, isn't it America's responsibility to do so?
6. Most languages are considered by their speech communities to be unique, at least in some ways or to some extent. Is this also true

about English? Should corpus planning for English try to make the language ever more unique?

7. What can be learned from the failures of most pan movements? Some African intellectuals are interested in creating or reviving a language for all sub-Saharan Blacks. What advice would you give them?

8. Do you know of any cases in which the resiliency or longevity of a small/weak language was actually curtailed precisely due to its great similarity to an essentially identical but much stronger language?

9. Can you think of any case in which speech-communities that practiced independence-focused corpus planning were actually more *dependent* on other polities than were the speakers of certain inter-dependence-focused, corpus-planning language at the same degree of separation?

10. Can both *Ausbau* and *Imbau* corpus planning be successfully implemented simultaneously? Give some examples of efforts to do so.

11. If you were the director of an authoritative corpus-planning agency, how would you go about creating and fostering the acceptance and use of new nomenclatures for interaction with communicative extraterrestrial intelligent life?

Extra-Credit 1: In what ways is Title VII bilingual education in the USA a case of corpus planning, status planning, both (in which case, is one type of language planning more necessary for bilingual education than the other?), or neither?

Extra credit 2: The following material (Appendix 2) is from a book (Rubin, J., Jernudd, B., Das Gupta, J., Fishman, J. A., & Ferguson, C., 1977. *Progress in Language Planning*. Mouton: New York, pp. 79–96) that was published much before the current book was even conceived of. Can any of the bipolar dimensions discussed *in the present volume* (and/or their related clusters) be recognized in connection with the data reported in the 1977 book? If so, are there any dimension(s) that are more common than others and are any missing entirely? Are there any additional dimensions that are suggested by the 1977 data?

Appendix 2

Jack Fellman and Joshua A. Fishman

A TERMINOLOGY COMMITTEE AT WORK*

Introduction

At the present time we know very little about the actual workings of the terminological committees so commonly set up by agencies concerned with language modernization. Alisjahbana alone (1960, 1971) devotes a few paragraphs to describing the work procedures of the Bahasa Indonesia terminology committees set up during the Japanese occupation of the former Dutch East Indies. Most other major reports of actual language planning or language modernization efforts—e.g., Haugen's re Norway (1966a, b), Heyd's re Turkey (1954), Kurman's re Estonian (1968), Al Toma's re Arabic (1969), Hamzaoui's re Arabic (1965), Guitarte and Quintero's re Spanish in Latin America (1968), Gastil's re Persian (1959), Whiteley's re Swahili (1969), Kirk-Greene's re Hausa (1964), Minn Latt's re Burmese (1966)—attend to the socio-political-

*From *Language Planning in Israel* by Jack Fellman and Joshua A. Fishman in *Language Planning Processes: Contributions to the Sociology of Language,* edited by Bjorn H. Jernudd, Joan Rubin, Jyotirindra Das Gupta, Joshua A. Fishman, and Charles A. Ferguson, 1977. The Hague, Mouton-de-Gruyter. Reprinted with permission.

cultural context of terminological innovation at best, and to a detailed examination of the finished product alone, at worst.

This study, therefore, focuses on the functioning of two terminological committees, in the hope that an examination of their procedures will not only be of direct interest but, also, will assist other scholars in formulating general questions concerning the operations of such committees. Hopefully, the time is not far off when the composition and procedures of such committees can be studied as variables that are themselves related to the nature of the products and, therefore, to the ultimate acceptability of the products that such committees produce.

CONSTITUTION AND COMPOSITION OF A COMMITTEE

Committee on the Terminology of Librarianship

The Hebrew Language Academy's Committee on the Terminology of Librarianship came into being as a result of a request from the Librarians' Association of Israel. The Association had appointed a small group of interested Librarians to provide Hebrew equivalents for the terms appearing in UNESCO's Terminology of Librarianship (*Vocabularuim Bibliothecarii*). After working at this task for a time, the group requested that the Association approach the Academy for assistance in completing the task. The Academy then delegated three of its staff members to serve on the Committee with the Association's representatives. The Academy also delegated one of its senior members to act as chairman of the joint committee. This procedure, although not an unusual one, was the reverse of the Academy's formalized procedure of purportedly taking the initiative in forming terminological Committees and then rounding out its own representation on such Committees with the most qualified specialists in the subject matter field under consideration. In the present case the Academy was quite willing to work with the individuals who hd been designated previously by the Librarians' Association, since these were among the most knowledgeable and important librarians of the country. Presumably the Academy could have insisted that other specialists of its choosing be added to the Committee had it not been perfectly satisfied with those already designated by the Librarians' Association.

The Academy's representatives on the Committee consisted of one its members who was a senior professor of Talmud at the Hebrew University and had already accumulated many years of experience on Committees of this kind, its two scientific secretaries and one of its junior members who served as the secretary to the Committee. Had the field under discussion been a more multifaceted one, the Committee's total membership, and particularly its specialized membership, would have been much larger. As it was the Committee consisted of nine people in all, five representing the Academy.

Committee on Terminology for Inorganic Chemistry

Twenty-some years ago the Hebrew Language Council dealt with the problem of coining Hebrew terminology for inorganic chemistry. The results of its deliberations were published in the Council's specialized journal *Leshonenu* and in due course entered suitable chemistry texts. However, the field of chemistry developed to such an extent in the ensuing 20 years that a new way of looking at chemical compounds had arisen, which demanded a new way of coining terms for various substances. Thus the Hebrew Language Council, now renamed Academy, felt it necessary to convene a Committee to discuss again matters of terminology in inorganic chemistry, not so much because the previous terminology had not been accepted in itself, but rather because it had been superseded. The Committee consisted of 11 members, of whom six represented the Academy. The chairman of the Committee was, as usual, an Academy representative. Once again he was a professor at the Hebrew University, but, this time, in chemistry rather than in a field more distant from the Committee's immediate task.

GENERAL WORK CYCLE

The Librarianship Committee met approximately 50 times over a three-year period. Initially it met every other week, but toward the end of its labors it met somewhat less frequently. After completing a preliminary translation of the UNESCO list of librarianship terms, the Committee distributed its first draft of recommended terms to a large list of librarians, members of the Academy and other interested parties. The coments received were reviewed by the Committee and a revised set of recommendations was prepared. This set, which included several split decisions, i.e., majority-backed and minority-backed recommendations, was then sent to all those who had responded with recommendations to the first draft, and further comments were requested. These were reviewed by the Committee and a full set of the Committee's recommendations was sent to the General Meeting (Plenum) of the Academy for its approval. The General Meeting in turn passed upon each term recommended by the Committee and in a very few instances asked the Committee to reconsider its recommendations. The Committee then prepared its final recommendations and the General Meeting accepted them after brief discussion.

Once accepted by the General Meeting the terminology was printed up in the customary small book or brochure format of Academy terminologies and distributed to all public libraries. Its recommendations were theoretically binding upon government libraries, once published in the government journal, since the Academy is recognized in law as the arbiter in language matters for all public, official purposes. Moreover, since the main librarians in the country served on the Committee and took an active role in the Committee's decisions it was assumed by all concerned that, even without the Academy's legal jurisdiction, its terminology as a whole would be accepted and used by the librarians of Israel. Depending on the rapidity of change within the field of librarianship itself, then, the terminology just completed will stand for a longer or shorter time, e.g., 5–20 years or more.

In part, the functioning of the Inorganic Chemistry Committee came under the regulation of a more recently instituted set of procedural regulations. Instead of bringing the Committee's recommendations directly to the General Meeting, where a terminological committee's work stood the chance of being criticized by Academy members who were not sufficiently familiar either with the technical field under consideration or with the compromises reached after months of painstaking work by the Committee members, these recommendations were brought to a General Committee on Terminology. This Committee consisted of three Academy members and three Academy staff, all individuals with long experience and very intense interest in problems of terminology. After a specific terminology was cleared by the General Committee on Terminology, a process which might well require more than one 'go-around' between the specific Committee and the General Committee, its subsequent final clearance by the General Meeting was considered to be a pro forma matter.

RECOLLECTED DIFFICULTIES

The difficulties recollected by the Committees' chairmen, after three years of work, were as follows.

Exhaustiveness

The UNESCO list is very long and includes many terms rarely used or required even by specialized librarians or chemists. An early difficulty, therefore, was to decided whether all or only some of the listed terms needed to be translated. It was finally decided that even if only one person needed an absolutely complete Hebrew terminology in librarianship or chemistry that was reason enough for preparing such a list. It was a mater of pride and conviction that the Hebrew list be fully inter-translatable with the UNESCO list (in English, French, German, and Russian), but this added greatly to the Committee's burdens.

Vintage

The choice between practice and perfection was another difficulty encountered by the Committees. Many terms were already well established in the usage of librarians and chemists. However, some of these terms were no longer fashionable among younger specialists. Others were felt not to be optimally good translations of corresponding UNESCO terms, particularly words in the list of definitions given to the latter in a standard handbook of librarianship terms (*The American Library Association Glossary of Library Terms*, prepared by Elizabeth H. Thompson, Chicago, 1943). Wherever possible the Librarianship Committee tried to go along with established usage among librarians but in a few cases it reluctantly decided against practice and opted for perfection instead.

Generation Gap

Related to the foregoing problem were the differences that often obtained between older and younger specialists, both among the Committees' own memberships as well as among the critics to whom their preliminary lists were distributed for comment. Older specialists were sometimes particularly loathe to set aside terms to which they were attached and accustomed. Thus, in the Chemistry Committee some wanted to keep terms they had learned in their youth, terms often modeled on French patterns. However, not only had chemistry changed but its use was now being modeled especially on English patterns.

Status differences also contributed to the difficulty sometimes experienced in accepting suggestions of younger members. No similar age-related differences were believed to obtain among the Academy-delegated members or Academy-related critics. The latter were recollected as having more unified views, this being attributed largely to their more unified linguistic orientations. Sometimes the Academy-delegated Committee members would help the Committee pass beyond an impasse between its older and younger specialist members by suggesting that a more final decision between two alternatives by left up to the General Meeting or the General Terminology Committee.

Academy Tradition

One of the major tasks of the Academy-delegated members was to keep in mind prior Academy terminologies as well as formal and informal policies and preference of the Academy or of its members who were likely to show up at a General Meeting. Academy-delegated members attempted to achieve consistency between the librarianship terminology and other terminologies approved by the Academy in recent years. They also tried to keep in mind the fact that some Academy members did not like certain morphemes, because they had been overused, and similar preferential tendencies that might cause difficulties when the Committee's recommendations came up for approval.

In the case of the Inorganic Chemistry Committee, it was decided at the very outset to fashion the terminology after the internationally accepted terms of the ICA (International Chemical Association), and, whenever problems arose, to follow the compounding pattern of the English-language term. Thus word order, for example, was to follow international order, which is not necessarily strictly Hebrew word order. Also, abbreviations, virtually lacking in Standard Hebrew, were to be adopted following international custom, for example, platin instead of platin*um*. A recurring problem in the Committee was the question of whether international chemistry roots, such as cobalt, phosphide, oxy-oxo-, were to be used in creating Hebrew terms. There were serious and continuing differences of opinion on this matter, not only within the Committee itself but within the General Terminology Committee as well.

Thank God

The Librarianship Committee chairman drew upon his experience with other Academy terminology committees in expressing his feeling of relief that librarianship was not marked by many highly specialized sub-fields with terminologies of their own, as is the case in chemistry. He was also grateful that librarianship was not in a rapid state of flux and that it was not polarized into different theoretical or applied camps. Finally, he considered it a blessing that librarianship was not a field in which some members were trained abroad, and, therefore, were accustomed to a high proportion of foreign lexical terms in their personal usage, which was another problem in chemistry. On the other hand, he felt that the specific UNESCO list was not a particularly good one. Its French and German equivalents had been prepared by Swiss librarians whose usage was not like that of 'real' French or 'real' German librarians. This often led the Hebrew Committee into fruitless byways and necessitated a great deal of checking with other references. The Chemistry Committee had far less trouble with work meanings, but far more difficulty with the coinage of new Hebrew equivalents for accepted international designations.

Specific Difficulties

After three years of work, certain terms remained unforgettably etched in the chairmen's minds because of the difficulty they had caused and e time they had consumed. Many of the most difficult terms were ones that existed in a complex conceptual relationship to others, so that shades of differences existed between them or they encompassed a number of different referents or operations in th source languages. One such word in Librarianship was 'entry', which could mean either *any* item on a list of titles, a full bibliographic description of an item in accord with a few standard criteria, etc. Very similar problems arose more frequently in the Chemistry Committee, since long lists of terms in conceptual relationship to each other are quite common in that field, e.g., -ide, -ite, -ate, -ous, -ic, etc.

RECURRING PROCEDURES

Sessions

The members of a Committee sit around a table, the center of which soon becomes cluttered with copies of the UNESCO list and other standard works on fields of terminological concern. From time to time other references, usually dictionaries, are taken from the shelves that line the walls and are consulted. Each member has a copy of the mimeographed list of terms under discussion at a particular meeting. The secretary also has all of the lists discussed at previous meetings so that it is possible to check for consistency with earlier recommendations. Each meeting lasts roughly three hours and covers approximately 50-60 problematic terms.

Handling Disagreement

In a large proportion of cases, agreement is reach among those seated around the table. Majority sentiment in favor of one suggestion or another is normally enough for minority recommendations to be abandoned. When this is not the case, the chairman or another member may sound out those assembled as to whether both of the alternatives might not be acceptable. If there is a serious objection to recommending two terms (and this does *not* seem to be a preferred solution) then both the majority and the minority recommendations are noted in the

minutes. It is generally understood that no committee can se
through a large number of split-decisions, and this awareness seen.
to be instrumental in keeping the number of minority recommendations at a low level.

The Thanks of the Academy

The final session of a committee's labors is a somewhat special occasion. The chairman, and the other Academy representatives, thank the
specialist members for their efforts and for their good work. The specialists are rather pleased that their work has finally come to an end, but
they say 'it was a pleasure' and 'let's hope the General Meeting ap-
proves', and 'may our work find favor in the eyes of our colleagues'. The
thanks of the Academy, ratification by the General Meeting, mention in
the official publication, and adoption in practice of the terminology proposed are the only rewards received by the specialist members of terminological committees of the Academy. Most of them will serve on no
other terminological committees for many years to come, if ever again.
For them, service on a committee of the Academy is expected to be its
own reward. It is an opportunity to interact with and to contribute to a
major national symbol which is not always respected but it is an aspect
of majesty none the less and few indeed will refuse to serve it when
called upon.

RECURRING QUESTIONS

What Does the Term Mean?

A frequent first question in connection with a term on the UNESCO list
was 'What is it? What does it refer to? What does it really mean?' Such
questions may necessitate considerable discussion and referrals to various reference works. On occasion, members are surprised to find that an
English word (or French word, etc.) which they have always used with a
particular meaning is defined as having another meaning or additional
meanings by other members or by the references consulted. Some examples of terms which provided definitional problems are: 'shared cata-
log', 'incipit', 'excipit', 'digest'.

ᴏ Suggested That?

The Committee members are all equal before the law but they are not equal in status or in each other's eyes. The suggestions and arguments advanced by some members received more careful and more sympathetic consideration than those advanced by others. This is also the case when written comments are received from outside critics. 'Who suggested that?' is a common question, and the reputation of the individual named functions as a halo effect in helping the questioner to interpret the intent and the merits of the suggestion or view under consideration.

What is the Academy's Position Re— ?

The substantive specialists on the Committee are, as a rule, lass familiar with the Academy's policies, preferences and positions. As a result, they more commonly ask for information along these lines and the Academy representatives more commonly offer unsolicited comments along these lines. For example, even though the Academy long ago expressed a preference for the use of indigenous Hebrew roots in the formation of new terms, a preference not considered binding in scientific fields, questions frequently arise about the acceptability of such-and-such an 'internationalism', 'Americanism', etc.

RATIONALES EMPLOYED

Almost invariably several alternative Hebrew terms are suggested, whether seriously or only half seriously. The choice among alternatives is then rationalized on one or more of the following grounds.

Intertranslatability: Fidelity to Source Language(s)

1. *taqqanon sifriyya* 'library statues' (1. rules. 2. regulations). One term was retained in Hebrew instead of two as in English, since in French there is only term, 'règlements'.

2. *tavnit qetana* 'miniature edition', was changed to *tavnit zeira*, as *zeira* translates 'miniature' more closely, and miniature is the form used in the English, French and German UNESCO equivalents.

3. *reshima* was kept over the proposed *ozar* because it more close᷈ corresponds to the corresponding English 'list' and French 'table'.

4. *sam sefer shelo bimekomo* 'to misplace a book' (involuntarily), was formed and retained as equivalent to the English, French (déplacer, malplacer un livre) and German (ein Buch verstellen).

In Chemistry terminology, the order of the Hebrew terms in the various compounds is, be necessity, the same order as the internationally accepted symbol-writing of the various elements. Thus in writing the term for water H_2O, the Hebrew for 'hydrogen' must precede the 'oxygen', even though Hebrew is written in the opposite direction from European-Latinate languages.

Consistency With Prior Recommendations

1. In *ones maksimali al harizpa* 'maximum floor load', *maksimali*, although of foreign provenience, was favored over the indigenously formed *meravi* as a legitimate Hebrew creation, the form having been coined by the public press and not by the Academy.

2. The spelling *arxiyonay* 'archival' although questioned, was kept, with full pointing of *o* in the Hebrew script, in accordance with Academy rules for spelling.

3. Thirty-four terms were all accepted en masse, as they ha already been prepared by the Academy Committee on (IBM) computer terminology, and had also been accepted en masse by a similar Academy Committee on photography.

4. The pronunciation of <n w s h> was questioned. Is it to be pointed and pronounced *nosah̲* or *nusah̲*? The Academy had previously decided *nosah̲* and such was entered.

5. The pointing and pronunciation of <m q v> was questioned and, according to Academy rules, *maqqev* was decided upon.

Desirable and Undesirable Typologies

Generally speaking the Librarianship Committee seemed to want to retain semantic distinctions, or lack of distinctions, were noted in the source languages. However, from time to time a strong rationale was ad-

ᴀnced on behalf of an indigenous typology, particularly if it was al-
ʀeady well established among local professionals.

1. *taqqanon* was kept for both the English (I) rules and (ii)
regulations, as the differentiation between the two words was not felt
necessary in librarianship, in distinction to law, for example.

2. *meshummash* was kept in Hebrew to mean both used and second-
hand instead of coining two terms as in the English, French and German 'used, thumbed; usagé, défraichi; mit Gebrauchsspuren, geb-
raucht'. It was not felt necessary to differentiate between the two in
librarianship.

Word or Phrase?

In some cases, phrases are recommended as the equivalents of single
words in the source language. Is this legitimate? There is the constant effort to translate a word by another word. Sometimes, however, a phrase
more fully meets the requirements of clarity, euphoniousness, etc.

1. *peteq lavay* 'process slip'. As this form is only used in
librarianship, it was felt that perhaps a short explanatory phrase
should be added, as in French and German (feuillet où l'on note les
diverses opérations don't un livre fait l'objet; Laufzettel für den Gag
des Buches).

2. *sam sefer shelo bimekomo* 'to misplace a book' (involuntarily)
was questioned as to whether it is a term for a dictionary or merely a
phrase. The decision was to retain it, as it corresponded to similar
phrases in the English, French and German equivalents.

3. Both the foreign *palimpsest* and the Hebrew phrase *ketav al
maḥaq* were retained.

Clarity, Unambiguity, Tranlatability to the Native Speaker

1. *keves* was changed to *deragrag* 'stepladder', because both the
root '*drg*' and the general noun form $C_1eC_2aC_3C_2aC_3$ are known more
generally than the term *keves*. The fact that there already exists a

related noun *sherafraf* 'footstool' also was used to gain Committee acceptance for the proposed form, as it was assumed the native speaker would easily relate the two.

2. Hebrew elements were favored over international ones in forming the various chemistry terms in order to facilitate learning on the part of the student. For the chemist, however, the international terms would seem to be more preferable, and thus a conflict arose over the extend to which the native speaker was to be considered in the Academy's decisions. For example, the form *natran-arba-okso-sulfati* 'sodium oxo-sulfatic (acid)', although acceptable to the chemist, might cause problems for the student who did not know the international terms *okso-* and *sulfati*. This being the case in general, the term was changed to *natran-arba-ḥamzan-gofriti*, with four native Hebrew terms.

Foreign Words-Roots/Native Words-Roots/One Term/ Several Terms?

1. Both indigenous Hebrew *mazhef* and foreign *codex* were given and retained in the list, to offer both a change to vie with one another in librarians' usage.

2. Both foreign *palimpsest* and the Hebrew phrase *ketav al maḥaq* were retained in the list, for similar reasons to those just mentioned. However it was questioned whether *palimpsest* should be written in Hebrew without the second p, as in English this p is not pronounced. However, the form was left as such, with no change.

3. Hebrew *geniza* was added to foreign *archiyon* 'archive'.

4. Both foreign *epigraf* and Hebrew *reshomet* were retained for 'epigraph'.

There is a general distaste in the culture with respect to the indiscriminate mixing of unlike elements. This distaste is summed up in the word *shaatnez* 'forbidden mixing', according to the Biblical prohibition of wearing a garment of mixed wool and cotton (Deuteronomy 22:11). In language we see this view expressed in the desire for either an all Hebrew or, if necessary, and all foreign term, but not a combination of the two. Thus, as above, *natran-arba-okso-sulfati*, although quite accept-able and useful for the scientist with its part Hebrew, part international root composition, was changed to the *all-Hebrew* form *natran-arba-ḥamẓan-gofriti*. Several Committee members commented that chemists would doubtlessly continue saying (but not writing) *Natran-es-oh-arba* sodium S-O-four).

The New is Old

Innovation proceeds primarily on the basis of established roots and in accord with established morphemic patterns. The lexical innovation is justified on the basis of the fact that it is in accord with the principles of accepted usage. If there is precedent for the new, particularly is the pre-cedent is Classical or Talmudic, then it is more easily justified.

1. In *kartis arai* 'temporary card', the spelling of *arai* was questioned as in Classical sources (Talmud Yerushalmi) and in manuscripts two different spellings are found. However, here the more commonly known spelling was retained.

2. The form *deragrag* 'stepladder', was chosen over the form *keves*, as the related verb form *dirdeg* in a similar meaning was found to exist in Geonic Responsa literature.

Appeal to 'Naive' Usage

How do ordinary librarians speak? How will ordinary librarians react to such and such? What do ordinary librarians mean by such and such? From time to time professional expertise is set aside and the librarian-in-the-street is appealed to, actually or in theory. On the other hand, the opposite is also done: the common librarian is considered to be a very unsuitable guidepost. For example, consider the term 'blurb'. Some ar-gued that 'blurb' pertained only to the publisher's brief words of praise on the book jacket itself. Others argued that the term also pertained to brief advertising material distributed by publishers or booksellers. Still others contended that any brief ad, even in a newspaper, was a blurb. In the midst of the discussion two visitors were appealed to. 'What does "blurb" mean to you?' they were asked. Their reply satisfied only a few of those present.

The Target Client Group

If the list of new terms is ultimately aimed at advanced professionals, such as chemists, then international roots can and should be used, since 'the scientific world as a whole is a unit, to which individual languages and linguistic customs must learn to comply'. This is felt, by some committee members, to be especially true for small, non-European nations and languages. Even if a new or revised terminology is ultimately aimed at university students rather than at the specialists per se, the international roots can be used, as these students will ultimately become the future specialists. However, if terminologies are aimed also, or even particularly, at the general public or at high school students and high school textbooks, then the roots employed should be Hebrew ones. The high school student generally does not know foreign languages and has ample time to learn them later, if he attends a university. Therefore, at the high school stage per se, emphasis should be wholly on content, i.e., on the new ideas being presented, and not on form. As a result, the terms employed should not be based on international or non-familiar roots but on native ones instead.

Unavoidable Internationalisms

In general the Chemistry Committee accepted and retained all Hebrew chemistry roots customarily in use, although actually there are only a small number of these. They also accepted all international roots customarily used in Hebrew and now felt to be part of Hebrew, for example, aluminium, caloric. However, there still remained to be considered many international roots and word-coinages which did not as yet exist in Hebrew, and it was decided to transfer them directly into the language rather than to translate them into Hebrew. Even then two questions of integration arose, namely the problems of affixation and transliteration.

The problem of affixation. It was decided that new foreign roots were to be considered fully integrated, and could combine with both other foreign roots and with native Hebrew roots. Older, established Hebrew roots in chemistry, however, were to combine only with other Hebrew roots. For example, the form *du-fosfidi* 'bi-phosphoric', is permissible, *du-* being considered part of the Hebrew (actually Aramaic) and *fosfidi* being considered international. Similarly, the form *heqsa-nitro-qobalti* 'sexta-nitro-cobaltic' is permissible, all three roots being considered international. However, the form *tetra-kalori* 'tetra-caloric' is inadmissible, as *kalori* is considered part of Hebrew (actually, of course, Greek, but found in the Mishna) and would have to be changed to *arba-kalori*, *arba-* being a Hebrew term. Sometimes, however, the all-Hebrew term, although acceptable and even desirable linguistically, came out conveying something undesirable, chemically speaking. Thus the chemists hit on the compromise position of Hebrew-*affixes* with foreign terms, as a linguistic device to obviate chemical inaccuracies. For example, the linguists/Academy members suggested *gofrit ẖamẕanit* for 'okso-sulphide'. Hebraically this is fine but chemically the form must be of the type *okso-gofrit*, i.e., where the salt, oxo-, *precedes* the acid, sulphide. The Hebrew-form on this pattern *ẖamẕano-gofrit* would be very forced – witness the o particle – and therefore was rejected, even by the Academy members, in favor of *okso-gofrit*, the hybrid, half-foreign, half-Hebrew term.

The problem of transliteration. It was decided that international terms which had already entered Hebrew and were felt to be part of the language as such were to continue in their already common Hebrew spelling. New international terms, however, would have to be fitted to the rules of the new Hebrew spelling devised by the Academy in the past three years. The pronunciation and spelling of the terms were to follow the parallel of the language from which the terms in question originally came; for example, francium pronounced and spelled with a soft *s* sound due to the parallel sound in la France, or, when not know or unsure, according to the Classical Latin pronunciation, for example, argentium pronounced and spelled with a hard *t*.

COMMENTS AND QUESTIONS

1. Do Academy members and associates recognize the above listed rationales as ones they have been using? Is there an order of preference for certain rationales over others? How do these rationales

compare to those of other Academies? Are particular rationales appealed to more/less in connection with certain fields that others?

A preliminary record such as the foregoing can be a point of departure not only for further observations but also for focused interviews with Academy members, staff and associates.

2. Do the rationales employed and decisions reached have an important relationship to the reception encountered by any particular nomenclature? Is the composition of the Committee and the work routine it uses of any importance in this connection? The full process records of many committees would be needed, as would a criterion of 'goodness of reception', before such questions could be answered.

3. Should an Academy, as a scientific body, explain how it selects or coins the various terms it publishes? For example, for each word of group of words in a terminological list, should sources and references be cited indicating or defending the validity of that term? A researcher has to do this in any journal article in which he introduces a neologism. In 1904 it was decided that only final results would be published in the Memoirs of the Hebrew Language Council (*Zikhronot Waad Ha-Lashon*), i.e., none of the arguments pro and con would be included. The Academy today is following the precedent of the *Waad Ha-Lashon* as well as following the course taken by other Academies. Would a contrary course materially alter the reception given to various terminologies? A process record, although not necessarily as detailed as that provided here, might be of interest to the intelligent reader and elicit his/her support for Academy decisions and recommendations.

SUMMARY AND CONCLUSIONS

A summary process record of the deliberations of two terminological committees of the Hebrew Language Academy reveals that there were both differences as well as similarities in their work procedures and in their substantive considerations. Internally, the two committee proceeded in much the same fashion; however, their structural relationship to the higher authority of the Academy was organized differently. This difference was related to a general desire to minimize future friction between individual terminology committees and the General Meeting of the Academy as a whole. The organizational change introduced as a result of this desire was made in time to effect the work of one committee (Inorganic Chemistry) but not the other (Librarianship).

Substantively the two committees grappled with quite similar problems and utilized very similar rationales in arriving at essentially similar compromise decisions. Although the problem of indigenousness/internationalness of terminology was far more severe in one field than in the other, both committees attempted more or less successfully to 'hold the line' in favor of indigenous or indigenized roots and constructions insofar as possible. Both reveal the recurring problem faced by language planning bodies constrained to pursue modernization within the general framework of an indigenous Great Tradition which frowns upon foreign influences in language if not in behavior.

REFERENCES

Alisjahbana, T. S.
  1960 *Indonesian Language and Literature: Two essays.* New Haven, Yale University Southeast Asia Studies.
——
  1971 'Some Planning Processes in the Development of the Indonesian/Malay Language', in *Can Language be Planned?*, ed. by J. Rubin and B. H. Jernudd. Honolulu, University of Hawaii Press.
Al-Toma, S. J.
  1969 'Language Education in Arab Countries and the Role of the Academies', pp. 690-720 in *Current Trends in Linguistics*, Vol. 6, ed. by T. A. Sebeok, The Hague, Mouton.
Gastill, R.
  1959 *Language Modernization: A Comparative Analysis of Persian and English Texts.* Cambridge, Mass., Center for International Affairs, Harvard University.
Hamzaoui, R.
  1959 *L'académie arabe de Damas et le problème de la modernisation de la langue arabe.* Leiden, Brill.
Haugen, E.
  1966a 'Linguistics and Language Planning', pp. 50-75 in *Sociolinguistics*, ed. by William Bright. The Hague, Mouton.
——
  1966b *Language Conflict and Language Planning. The Case of Modern Norwegian.* Cambridge, Harvard University Press.
Heyd, U.
  1954 *Language Reform in Modern Turkey.* Jerusalem, Israel Oriental Society.

Kirk-Greene, A. H. M.
   1964 'The Hausa Language Board', *Afrika und Uebersee* 47: 187-203.
Kurman, G.
   1968 *The Development of Written Estonian* (*Indiana University Publications: Uralic and Altaic Series* 90). The Hague, Mouton.
Minn Latt, Y.
   1966 *Modernization of Burmese*. Prague, Oriental Institute, Academia Publishing House of the Czechoslovak Academy of Sciences.
Whitley, W. H.
   1969 *Swahili: The Rise of a National Language*. London, Methuen.

References[1]

(Cited Works)*

Celan, P. (2004). *Todesfuge und andere Gedichte*. Suhrkamp: Frankfurt A. M.

Churchill, W. S. (1908). The joys of writing. In *Complete Speeches, 1897–1963* (Vol.1, p. 904). New York/London: Bowker. R. R. James (Ed.). (Reprinted in Joshua A. Fishman, 1996)

Cruz, I. (1991). A nation searching for a language finds a language searching for a name. *English Today, 7*, 17–21.

Despalatović, E. M. (1975). *Ljudevit Guy and the Illyrian movement*. Boulder: Eastern European Quarterly.

Department of Education, Culture and Sports and Institute of Philippine Languages. (1991). *Primer on executive order no. 335*. Manila: Philippine Information Agency.

Durkheim, E. (2003). *Sociologist of modernity*. M. Emirbaye (Ed.). Malden: Blackwell.

Fishman, J. A. (1963). Nationality-nationalism and nation-nationism. In J. A. Fishman, C. A. Ferguson, & J. Das Gupta (Eds.), *Language problems of developing nations* (pp. 39–52). New York: Wiley.

Fishman, J. A. (1996). *In praise of the beloved language* (pp. 206–207). Berlin, Mouton de Gruyter.

---

[1]The best single collection of international corpus-planning examples is to be found in the several volumes edited by Fodor, Istvan, & C. Hagege (1983–1994), *Language reform: History and future*. Hamburg: Buske.

The more recent literature, particularly that in English, can be followed (and abstracts obtained) by consulting the *LLBA* data-base (formerly *Language and Language Behavior Abstracts*, now *Language and Linguistics Abstracts*).

* Plus some further recommended readings. No attempt has been made to cite the worldwide status planning literature.

Fishman, J. A. (1980). Bilingual education, language planning and English. *English Worldwide, 1,* 11–24.

Fishman, J. A. (1983). Modeling rationales in corpus planning: Modernity and tradition in images of the good corpus. In J. Cobarrubias & J. A. Fishman, (Eds.), *Progress in language planning* (pp. 107–118). Berlin: Mouton.

Fishman, J. A. (1996). *In praise of the beloved language.* Berlin: Mouton.

Fishman, J. A. (Ed.). (2001). *Can threatened languages be saved?* Clevedon: Multilingual Matters.

Fishman, J. A. (2004). Yiddish and German; An on-again, off-again relationship (and some of the more important factors determining the future of Yiddish). In A. Gardt & B. Huppauf (Eds.), *Globalization and the future of German* (pp. 213–227). Berlin: Mouton.

Fishman, J. A., & Cobarrubias, J. C. (Eds.). (1983). *Progress in language planning.* Berlin: Mouton.

Fishman, J. A., Conrad, A., & Rubal-Lopez, A. (Eds.). (1996). *Post-imperial English: Change in the status of English, 1940–1990, in former British and American colonies and spheres of interest.* Berlin: Mouton de Gruyter.

Fishman, J. A. (in press). Yiddish language planning and standardization. *The YIVO Encyclopedia of Jews in Eastern Europe.*

Ford, C. (2002). Language planning in Bosnia and Herzegovina: The 1998 Bihac Symposium. *Slavic and Eastern European Studies, 46*(2), 349–361.

Gonzalez, A. (1980). *Language and nationalism: The Philippine experience thus far.* Quezon City: Ateneo de Manila University Press.

Greenberg, R. D. (2004). *Language and identity in the Balkans: Serbo-Croat and its disintegration.* New York: Oxford University Press.

Hall, R. A. (1950). *Leave your language alone!* Ithaca: Linguistica.

Helgi, V., & Ribenis, K. (2000). *Johannes Aavik and Estonian language Innovation: Bibliography, 1901–1996.* Tallinn: Akadeemia Truk.

Hornjatkjevyč, A. (1993). The 1928 Ukrainian orthography. In J. A. Fishman (Ed.), *The Earliest Stage of Language Planning* (pp. 293–304). Berlin: Mouton.

Hughes, R. (1920). Our Statish language. *Harper's Magazine,* 846–849. (Reprinted in J. A. Fishman, 1996)

Kloss, H. (1993). *Abstand* languages and *Ausbau* languages. *Anthropological Linguistics, 35,*(1–4), 158–170. (Original work published 1967)

Kohn, H. (1944). *The idea of nationalism: A study in its origins and background.* New York: Macmillan.

Landau, J. (1993). The first Turkish language congress. In J. A. Fishman (Ed.), *The Earliest Stage of Language Planning* (pp. 271–292). Berlin: Mouton.

Landau, J. (1984). *Ataturk and the modernization of Turkey.* Boulder: E. J. Brill.

Llamzon, T. (1996). A requiem for Pilipino. In B. P. Sibayan & A. Gonzalez (Eds.), *Language planning and the building of a national language: Essays in honor of Santiago A. Finacier on his 92nd birthday.* Manila: University of the Philippines and Philippine Normal College.

McCully, B. T. (1940). *English education and the origins of Indian nationalism.* New York: Columbia University Press.

McFarland, C. (1998). English enrichment of Filipino. *Philippine Journal of Linguistics, 29*, 73–90.

Molee, E. (1888). *Plea for an American language or Germanic English.* Chicago: Anderson.

Molee, E. (1894). *Pure Saxon English or American to the front.* Chicago and New York: Rand McNally.

Rogger, H. (1960). *National consciousness in eighteenth-century Russia.* Cambridge: Harvard University Press.

Ross, A. S. (1938). Artificial words in present-day Estonian. *Transactions of the philological society,* London, 64–72.

Rozniak, Z. (1988). Bilingualism and bureaucratism. *Nationalities Papers, 16*(2), 260–271.

Schaechter, M. (1977). Four schools of thought in Yiddish language planning. *Michigan Germanic Studies, 3*(2), 34–66.

Schiffman, H. (1996). *Linguistic culture and language policy.* New York: Routledge.

Stavans, I. (2003). *Spanglish: The making of a new American language.* New York: Rayo.

Veski, J. V. (1902). *Eesti Kirjakeele reeglid.* Tallinn.

Wines, M. (2002, April 18). Russia resists plans to tweak the mother tongue. *New York Times,* lgpolicy-list@ccat.sas.upenn.edu

Zhigang, X. (2004, September 13). Purity of Chinese language debated. *China Daily,* p.1.

Zuckerman, G. (2003). *Language contact and lexical enrichment in Israeli Hebrew.* New York: Palgrave Macmillan.

Author Index

Subject Index

Note: Pages numbers ending in "f" refer to figures; numbers ending in "t" refer to tables.